THE MEANING OF LIFE

IN FIVE GREAT RELIGIONS

THE MEANING OF LIFE
IN FIVE GREAT RELIGIONS

1344   EDITED BY

R. C. CHALMERS AND JOHN A. IRVING

The Westminster Press
Philadelphia

Library of Congress Catalog Card No. 66-10961

Published by The Westminster Press ®
Philadelphia, Pennsylvania

PRINTED IN THE UNITED STATES OF AMERICA

FOREWORD

The five great religions dealt with in this book have a long history, with many traditions behind them. In former days these religions have been relatively isolated from one another. However, in this age in which modern methods of communication and transportation have made the world into one "global village" the old isolation has been brought to an end. Buddhist and Christian, Muslim and Jew, Hindu and agnostic, intermingle socially and academically every day in many countries of the world.

This new situation constrains people of the various faiths to try to understand each other and especially to know what other persons believe about the great issues of life and destiny. The one world of today has compelled the leaders of these faiths to enter into an ecumenical dialogue in order to promote better understanding, to clarify basic problems and to further the interests of world community.

The purpose of this book is to make a contribution to this dialogue between five world religions and to centre the discussion on the meaning of life which, we believe, is a fundamental question in all religions.

When this book was ready for the press, word was received of the sudden death of one of the editors, Professor John A. Irving, Victoria College, University of Toronto, who was associated with the undersigned from the beginning in the preparation of this book. A man of broad learning and wise judgment, a splendid teacher and scholar, Professor Irving will be greatly missed in academic and other circles. We wish to record our sincere thanks and appreciation of the life and work of so valued a friend.

Pine Hill Divinity Hall,   R. C. CHALMERS
Halifax, N.S.
February 22, 1965.

CONTENTS

W. S. TAYLOR

I. ENCOUNTER

To say that a Christian should love his neighbour is to use a platitude. To say that the Christian should love the Hindu, the Buddhist or the Muslim is to use words that might become fighting words, depending on how close and irritating the encounter between Christian and non-Christian has been. Yet the two statements are virtually synonymous, since modern technological developments have destroyed the traditional correlation between geographical distance and psychological distance.

Only half a century ago, G. K. Chesterton could make pointed comments about the ease with which love for a distant foreigner, who was too far away to be disturbing, could be substituted for the difficult task of loving one's immediate neighbour:

Before any modern man talks with authority about loving men, I insist (I insist with violence) that he shall always be very much pleased when his barber tries to talk to him. His barber is humanity; let him love that. If he is not pleased at this, I will not accept any substitute in the way of interest in the Congo or in the future of Japan.[1]

The significant point now is, of course, that the African in the Congo and the Buddhist in Japan are almost as close as one's barber.

This is fairly obvious. It is also fairly obvious that, if the Hindu of India, the Buddhist of Japan, and the Muslim of Africa have become neighbour to the Christian, he must learn to love them. But if it is obvious, it is not easy. Psychological closeness can magnify the irritations caused by differences in outlook, custom, belief and tradition, without correspondingly magnifying the lovable qualities. One needs to remember that

---

[1] G. K. Chesterton: *Tremendous Trifles*. Methuen. 10th edition, 1927. p. 138.

Christian love is not the same thing as liking; not even the same as affection. It can be practised where there is neither liking nor affection; but it cannot be practised effectively at a psychological distance.

On this simple principle Florence Allshorn began in 1941 the first of the communities that have made her name and influence so notable in Christian circles. Her first community was in a house in Haslemere where a group of women were dedicated to the task of learning how to love each other by sharing a common kitchen, even if they never did learn wholly to like each other. It demonstrated that the finest Christian virtue must flower in the soil of difficult, close contact. Communities which began as a form of discipline for a group of women have now become places where controversial protagonists of differing views may gather and learn how to speak in honesty with love. The principle which has been worked out in such small communities must now be worked out also in the greater encounter between Christianity and other faiths. This is our opportunity.

When the International Missionary Council met in Jerusalem in 1911 it could look out on a world which was divided, traditionally, into differing spheres of religious influence. Buddhism, in its various forms, claimed the loyalty of people in Southeast Asia and Japan, but not the loyalty of people in Africa, Europe or the Americas. Hinduism claimed the minds of most people in India, but made no serious attempt to claim the minds of people in Europe or America. Both looked on Christianity as properly the religion of the west. Only Christianity and Islam, recognizing no such comity of religious areas, planned to move into places which others felt were their own.

Today, little more than half a century later, the picture has completely changed. There is no longer any recognized comity of religious influence. A boy or a girl growing up in the Americas finds the claims of Buddhism, Hinduism or Islam presented to him in various ways, as well as the claims of Christianity. When Buddhists point out how frequently Christianity seems to have led the west into war, and when the Attorney-

General of Burma says that "Buddhism is the only ideology which can give peace to the world," he is speaking to young people of the west as well as to young people of Burma. When a government spokesman in Rangoon says that "freedom is being threatened by a sinister ideology (Communism) and we are convinced that Buddhism can stem the tide," young people growing up in Europe may note that, in Burma, a sharp decrease of support for Communism has, in fact, accompanied the renascence of Buddhism, and may wonder if there is some justification for the spokesman's claim.

While modern methods of communication have made the claims of Hinduism and Buddhism known to Christian and Muslim young people in Europe, Africa and the Americas, they have also changed the attitudes of Hindus and Buddhists themselves. When Mahatma Gandhi left India to go to England for studies, he was made outcaste by the Hindu community to which he belonged, on the grounds that religion did not permit such travel. The community felt it belonged to a certain area; had adopted a total organization of human life, including diet and public health, which it could maintain within the area; and protected its monopoly by barriers against travel. Today, an acknowledged spokesman of the new Hinduism like Sir S. Radhakrishnan, who has been called the Ambassador-General of Indian Culture, can say that all attempts on the part of the historical religions to regain universality are bringing them closer to the point of view of the religions of India, and that the mystical insights of Hinduism are likely to provide the norms for the religion of the future. Today the new Buddhism also has become a religion with a sense of obligation to penetrate the west and save it from itself. One of the tasks set before itself by the Sixth Ecumenical Conference of Buddhists, held in Burma from 1954 to 1956, was to prepare a selection of the Buddhist scriptures, and a pattern of evangelism, which would make possible a missionary thrust into the Christian west.

The old concept of religious spheres of influence has disappeared both in fact and in principle. The major religions now recognize no territorial limits. They all base their claims on a capacity to meet universal human need. They all claim the right to enter into dialogue with each other, even into controversy and conflict, wherever and whenever they may meet. For perhaps the first time since the rise of Islam in the seventh century of the Christian era, Christianity must meet other religions face to face, anywhere and everywhere, in open competition for the minds of men. This is bound to have far-reaching effects, on formulations of Christian theology, on methods of Christian apologetic, on programmes of Christian education, and even on ecclesiastical polity. The last half of the twentieth century may become one of the great creative periods of Christian thought. The Christian may well thank God that he is permitted to live in a time like this, and to make his contribution, however small it may seem, to this process.

Two points can now be clearly stated.

The first is that the present free encounter between the great religions of the world should be welcomed by Christians rather than deplored. Christianity has always opposed regional spheres of influence, and has maintained the right to enter into free encounter with other faiths wherever it can meet them. It is quite in accordance with this principle that the encounter should take place on the home ground of the Christian, as well as on the home ground of the Buddhist, or Hindu or Muslim. In arguing that there should be no territory which is the private preserve of any religion, Christians are at the same time maintaining that there is no territory which is the private preserve of Christianity. The Christian cannot, on the one hand, throw a spiritual curtain around so-called Christian countries, to stop other religions at its borders, while refusing to recognize the right of other faiths to do the same. The Christian must be prepared to do unto others as he is willing to have them do unto him.

In fact the Christian can look on the willingness of Hinduism, for instance, to give up all claim to be an ethnic religion, as a first triumph for a principle which he considers fundamental.

4

The emergence of other great religions as competitors of Christianity on the basis of their capacity to meet man's spiritual needs is important. It means that the dialogue of religions is being started on grounds which already acknowledge a principle for which Christianity has argued.

The second point is that this new encounter of religions provides the Christian with a special opportunity to practise what he claims as a primary virtue of his faith. Grace and truth, says the writer of the Gospel of John, came by Jesus Christ. It is the peculiar combination of grace with truth which is significant. Mere truth by itself is less than Christian: mere truth which will let the chips fall where they may, and shows no love. Mere grace by itself is less than Christian: grace which is willing to trifle with truth because of its innate kindliness. Truth-with-grace and Grace-with-truth: this is the only attitude the Christian can rightfully practise. We can paraphrase it as honesty-in-love. And what better place to practise it than in the encounter of world religions?

This matter is so important that we must return to it later. Meanwhile we must move on to other things. So far we have been speaking particularly of the point of view of the Christian in this dialogue of religions. It is time now to consider problems which representatives of all religions must face, each in his own way.

One of the most important of these arises out of the tension, which each of the great religions faces, between the claim to uniqueness and finality for itself as over against other religions, and the obligation to share common concerns with them; between the obligation to stand against them and the obligation to stand with them, against common enemies; between the duty of exclusiveness and the duty of inclusiveness.

The relative emphasis given to each of these may vary greatly from one religion to another, though both are present. Orthodox Islam, for example, lays primary emphasis on the uniqueness and finality of the Qur'anic revelation. Though revelation through the Bible is recognized, it is preparatory and needs correction. Christ is considered to be related to Mohammed, in Muslim thought, much as John the Baptist is to Christ in Christian thought. The claims to revelation made by religions other than the Judaeo-Christian have not even this degree of validity. They are to be rejected. Yet even Islam, which is one of the most intransigent of all religions in its claims to uniqueness, has throughout the centuries clearly recognized an obligation to work with members of other faiths in implementing the requirements of its canon law for administrative and welfare purposes.

Hinduism, on the other hand, has placed its primary emphasis on the other pole, that of inclusiveness. It has claimed to be the most hospitable of all religions, eager to recognize the truth in every religious point of view, able to include within its hospitable embrace whatever other religions had to offer. Yet even Hinduism makes claims to uniqueness. It claims to be the only world religion capable of being so embracingly hospitable. In this sense it sets itself over against others as the only religion capable of transcending them in the very act of absorbing them.

In Christianity, however, this tension is found in an acute form. The problem of formulating his attitude to other religions is therefore a peculiarly perplexing and difficult problem for the thoughtful Christian.

By the very nature of his faith, the Christian is inextricably involved in healing the broken-hearted and the blind, in feeding the hungry, in clothing the naked, in caring for the sick, the captive and the homeless. Involvement in programmes of public health, education, medical care, nutrition, refugee relief, etc., is an essential part of the Christian's expression of the Gospel, and not an expendable supplement to it: much less a subtle public relations technique to soften people to the Gospel, as has sometimes been suggested. In carrying out such programmes the Christian can occasionally keep both the planning and operation in his own control. Generally, however, he must be prepared to surrender exclusive control, and accept the status of one participant along with others. In the fight against hunger and disease, for instance, modern methods of prevention, diagnosis and treatment all require a high degree of intercultural communication, planning and co-operative practice. Unilateral action by one religious or cultural group alone won't work.

The very nature of the Christian's obligation to care for the suffering and the needy requires him to sit down in partnership with non-Christians willing to work for common objectives. In this area the Christian ideal imposes on the Christian a policy of partnership with men of other faiths.

On the other hand the Christian also believes that the revelation of God in Christ Jesus is unique and final. On this particular matter there can be no simple partnership with people of other faiths.

The tension between these two points of view involves the ordinary thoughtful Christian in real perplexity. On Friday he sits around a table with fellow doctors, fellow economists, or fellow educators, in a partnership of mutual respect, to plan co-operatively for the attack on illness, hunger or poverty. On his right may be a Buddhist, on his left a Muslim, and across from him a Hindu. He feels that this is a right relationship. On Sunday he goes to church and is reminded that the Buddhist, Muslim and Hindu colleagues who sat with him are religiously in error, and that the Christian's duty is to convert them to the truth. He can hardly help feeling that his mental gears have been shifted from forward to reverse. He can hardly help wondering if the Church's attitude may, perhaps, be an outmoded hangover from the past. And yet, in his heart, he knows that the Church is right to maintain the unique finality of God's revelation in Christ.

The thoughtful Christian finds himself with two seemingly incompatible attitudes, both of which seem to him to be Christian. He is right. They *are* both Christian. But while both attitudes are Christian, either of them taken by itself, in isolation, is less than Christian. When either attitude is maintained as an alternative which is incompatible with the other, it is maintained in a way which makes it false. Both are necessary. The problem is to discover the pattern of thinking which will enable one to hold them together without their being mutually destructive.

Two things can be said about this situation.

The first is merely a reminder of what has already been said, namely, that the encounter must always be in the spirit of what the New Testament calls *agape,* or love. It is not necessary to agree with another person in order to show him this kind of love. It is possible to disagree radically with his religious views, to think him foolishly, even disastrously, wrong in his religious beliefs, and still to love him. What makes fellowship difficult, and puts the greatest strain on love, is a suspicion of hypocrisy rather than a suspicion of disagreement.

The second is to be sure we understand what the Sunday attitude really involves. For the Christian to believe that his colleague from another religion is wrong, even disastrously wrong, in his religious views does not give the Christian any right to look down on him. The Christian, whose sole hope is in the grace of God, cannot look down on anyone. The Christian who believes that, though men are sinners, they were not destroyed by the just wrath of God but saved by his terrible love and brought into the very household of God, cannot keep others beyond a curtain of condemnation because he believes their views are wrong. "God was in Christ reconciling the world unto himself," said St. Paul. The Christian can follow no other plan. But reconciliation does not work by anathemas, and it does not work from a distance; it works by participating with the person who is wrong. In a real sense, therefore, what was described as the Sunday attitude is so far from being the antithesis of the Friday attitude that it actually requires the Friday attitude as its proper complement.

Once we recognize that the supposed opposition between the Friday attitudes of partnership and the Sunday claims to uniqueness may be a false opposition, we are led directly into a consideration of principles governing this encounter of religions which must be faced by all parties equally. Studying them will lead us into semi-philosophical problems. For the supposed antagonism between different points of view often grows out of habits of thinking which operate unconsciously, and which form the unacknowledged presuppositions of one's understanding. The presuppositions with which thinking starts have a profound effect on the kind of conclusion at which one arrives. When an ordinary citizen of Europe or America, for instance, whose presuppositions are still formed by the cause-and-effect relationships of nineteenth-century science, studies the problem of pain, he almost inevitably reaches conclusions which deal with the causes of pain. When an orthodox Hindu or Buddhist, whose presuppositions are not formed by nineteenth-century cause-and-effect theories, similarly looks at the problem of pain, his conclusions may deal with the symbolic meaning of pain. Each of them finds the other's position mystifying because neither of them has allowed for the influence of the unconscious presuppositions of his thought. Good, sound understanding of a problem always requires us to bring these presuppositions out into the light, examine them, and allow for their influence. This is what we must try to do.

The habits of thinking which form unconscious presuppositions in the study of world religions cluster around the problem of classification. This may sound abstract and uninteresting. It will, I hope, become more meaningful as we try to illustrate it.

Without quite realizing what we are doing, we may adopt any one of four different methods of classification in trying to get the phenomena of world religions into intelligible relation with each other.

The first is the method of classification by dichotomous division which has become almost second nature to us under the influence of modern science, particularly biological science. By this, things are divided into two mutually exclusive groups, which can again be sub-divided into other mutually exclusive groups. They can be divided, for instance, into animate and inanimate. Animate things can further be divided into vertebrate

9

and invertebrate, and the vertebrate further divided into viviparous and oviparous. The same method of classification can be applied to social and cultural things, as well as religious. It was expressed, for instance, in the statement made frequently about the time of the Tambaram Conference of the International Missionary Council, that between Christian belief and non-Christian belief there was no point of contact, i.e., that they were mutually exclusive. It is expressed in the theological position that between God's revelation and all human religion there is no point of contact. It implies that the lines of distinction are sharp and clear, without any significant overlap.

The problem in using this type of classification is to make sure that the phenomena of religious experience and belief really do satisfy these conditions. The danger of this type of classification is that it may pander unconsciously to a desire to see everything in one's own group as good, and everything outside it as inferior.

The second is the method of classification by genus and species. Its title sounds pretentious, but in fact it is very simple and common. Its roots go so far back, through our traditions into Greek thought, that it has become an unconscious presupposition of much of our thinking to a greater extent even than the previous method. Illustrations abound. Trees which we call pines form a genus or class with the name *Pinus*. Included in this class are many species which we popularly call white pine, red pine, ponderosa pine, jack pine, etc. Each of these subordinate types possesses some common characteristics which it shares with all the other species belonging to this genus, while each possesses also some distinctive features of its own. The same method of classification can be used with cultural things. Music is a genus which has many different species of music grouped under it. The same holds true for painting, drama or literature, for government, association and family. It is frequently used in studies of the religions of the world. When this happens, the different religions are thought of as being different species, more or less on the same level, of a common genus to

10

which they all belong, namely, religion-in-general, or universal religion. Where this method is used without conscious recognition of what it involves, one can find oneself adopting beliefs about religion-in-general without quite knowing why one is doing so.

Three features of this kind of classification need to be recognized. (1) It tends to say "both-and" rather than "either-or," and to be syncretistic in general emphasis. (2) Though it recognizes both the common qualities belonging to the genus, and the differentiating properties of each species, it tends to exaggerate the importance of the genus qualities, and to play down the importance of the distinctive features of each species. In the religious sphere, this means exaggerating the importance of the common features which all religions share, and postulating a universal or general religion of which each religion is a minor form. (3) The particular characteristics of each religion tend to be treated as individual elements which can be isolated from the total pattern of that religion, and compared with similar characteristics drawn from other religions, as, for instance, the bone-structure in the wing of any one species of swallow could be compared with the similar bone-structure in the wing of any other species of swallow. In the study of religion it may be held, for instance, that a belief in God is a common feature of all religions, or in life after death, or a belief in spirits, or a belief in the need for salvation.

With this method of classification, as with the first, it is very important that one should examine religious beliefs and practices with scrupulous honesty to see if they really do lend themselves, without distortion, to this kind of classification. Where each religion is a complex whole of interrelated parts, is it true that a single part can be isolated from the rest without serious loss, or is every part so coloured by the whole pattern of which it is a part that it cannot be isolated without losing something essential to its nature? Can the Hindu view of God and the Muslim view of God be isolated and set side by side for comparison, or do they each reflect necessarily qualities of the total pattern to which they belong? Can the Muslim view of the mercy of Allah, and the Christian view of the mercy of God, be isolated for comparison with each other, or do they each reflect the qualities of the total ideological pattern in which they belong? Can the Hindu view of salvation, and the Christian view of salvation, be isolated for comparison without also taking account of their differing views of the place of man in the universe? These are major points at issue in modern studies of religion.

It is interesting to speculate on the extent to which various religions themselves emphasize these two points of view. Does orthodox Islam, with its insistence on the radical discontinuity between Qur'anic revelation and all religions which are non-Abrahamic in origin, build on the first method of classification? Does Hinduism, with its claim that at heart all religions are one, emphasize the second?

It may turn out that the phenomena of religion can not be dealt with adequately by either of these methods of classification, and there are other kinds of classification still to be considered.

R. G. Collingwood noted that many of the things we value most are too subtle in their nature, and overlap too much in their complex relationships, to be amenable to classification by either of the previous two methods. He suggested that philosophy might have to pay more attention to classification in terms of a norm and of approximations to a norm. H. H. Farmer, in his Gifford lectures, argued that this was the proper method to use in any study of religions. It is a method with which we are most at home in the areas of moral philosophy and of aesthetics, though it is not by any means limited to these fields. The norm provides the standard in terms of which all the phenomena are judged; the phenomena are judged in terms of their approximation to, or deviation from, the standard; and this measure of approximation to, or deviation from, the standard, in turn provides the ground on which various religious phenomena can be compared with each other. The norm is a necessary part of the total system, but it never exists on a basis of equality with any other parts of the system. All other elements share a common reference to the norm, but differ in their degree of approximation to it. In a peculiar sense, the norm is both immanent in, and transcendent to, the system, both at the same time.

This may sound complicated when stated in abstract form, but is in fact a method of classification that we use all the time. In morals we readily accept the idea of a norm of perfect truth, and judge individual statements by the way in which they approximate to it. In all forms of co-ordinated activity, we postulate a standard of perfect co-ordination, and try to judge each individual effort by its degree of approximation to this norm. In current theology, it may be found in the insistence of some theologians that the revelation of God in Christ is an absolute norm which must be clearly distinguished from any credal statements or Church practices, and that any theological statement, Christian or non-Christian, must be judged by its approximation to this norm, or its deviation from it.

It does not take a great deal of imagination to see how readily a method of classification like this could be used in a study of the religions of the world. What remains obscure is the method by which an acceptable norm is to be established. This may prove to be a focal point in the dialogue of religions.

This very difficulty leads into the consideration of the final method of classification which must be considered. It is difficult to give it, as yet, a special name, though its presence can be recognized in a wide range of contemporary thought. It might, perhaps, be described as a method of classification by challenge and response, or by presentation and perception, or by revelation and interpretation. It always involves a presentation and a response to the presentation, something which is given, and man's attempt to deal with what is given by patterns of action and belief. Differences in the nature of the response determine the classification. It will be readily recognized that differences in the nature of the response may not be reducible simply to different degrees of approximation to a standard along a common line of behaviour. If different deer of the same species all react to a common danger by flight, there may be differences in the speed and effectiveness of the flight. This would represent differences in degree for the same kind of response. But if the response of different creatures to a common danger is sometimes attack, sometimes flight, and sometimes "freezing," the responses move in different directions, though all respond to a common presentation. It is possible that this will prove a pattern applicable to the study of religions.

The fact that different people interpret the same presented material in quite different ways has now been established by such a wide range of experimental and clinical observations that it does not need supporting evidence here. It has become one of the major bases of personality diagnosis, carrying over into the field of cultural anthropological studies. Its application to the study of religion is both obvious and suggestive. The writer of the book of Job and Gotama Buddha were both presented with the fact of inescapable, even though unmerited, suffering; but their interpretations of the nature of the problem, and their responses to it, were different. Men of all religions are presented with the inescapable facts of death; but their interpretations of the significance of this fact, and the patterns of thought and behaviour based on their interpretations, are quite different. Between the Hindu doctrine of cycles of rebirth, the Christian doctrine of a resurrection body, and the Buddhist doctrines of Nirvana and Anatta, there are great differences; yet they all grow out of responses to the same presented problem. The student of religions will find many more illustrations of the same point.

It will be apparent that the latter two methods of studying religions avoid some of the weaknesses of the former two methods, and open up exciting possibilities. They also create new problems of their own. Classification by a norm and approximations to the norm raises immediately the question of how the validity of the norm is to be determined. Classification by variety of response to a common presentation at once raises a question as to how the adequacy of the various responses, and the validity of their accompanying beliefs, are to be determined.

It may be helpful to recognize at the outset that, in the tradition of western thought alone, a number of different methods have been used to test the validity of a belief.

One method is to check a belief, and its implications, by its correspondence with objective facts. One might call it the test of actuality. In ordinary experience we do this all the time. If I believe there is someone downstairs in the house, I test the validity of this belief by going down to see if there really is someone there. Scientific studies require a constant checking of belief against controlled, experimental observation; and though the scientific observation of fact now requires very complex and sensitive instruments, and though the objective facts as science understands them tend to make nonsense of ordinary everyday observations, the principle of the method remains. But there is much in the field of religion that does not seem to lend itself readily to this kind of check. The belief that God exists is hardly amenable to verification by observation, nor the belief that the poor shall inherit the earth, nor the belief in Nirvana, nor beliefs in revelation, to select only a few examples of religious belief.

A second method of testing the validity of a belief is the test of logical coherence within the whole system to which it belongs, a method which is very natural to philosophy, and which plays a big part in the development of scientific theories. One might call it the test of truth. The long history of western thought amply demonstrates, however, that the most logically coherent system can be no truer than the premises on which it is based.

A third method of checking the validity of beliefs might be called a test of their reality. It has come into particular prominence during the past half-century, under the impact of psychoanalytic studies. It draws its meaning from the antithesis of reality and fantasy thinking. To explain its general purport, one cannot do better than to go back to Freud's own explanation

15

of it, as it bore on religious questions. Whether or not religious beliefs correspond with any objective facts, he said, is of secondary importance. What they do to our wishful thinking is what is really important about them. Each man lives out his life in a sort of dialectical tension between his own personal wishes and the unchangeable life-situation in which he is placed. His life-situation is full of things he cannot wholly foresee, and cannot eliminate or remodel to suit his own convenience. These constitute Reality. Reality thinking means thinking which takes adequate account of these unchangeable realities of life, without misinterpreting and distorting them to suit one's personal desires. On this view, when one asks about the reality of religious beliefs, he is in effect asking: how well do these beliefs help one to face up honestly, courageously and creatively to the inescapable facts of life? In the dialectical back-and-forth interaction between personal desire and what St. Paul called the "necessities of life," how well do religious beliefs help one to avoid comfortable fantasies in favour of a mature realism? Life is a process in which we are repeatedly presented with aspects of reality, in which we perceive and partially misinterpret them in accordance with our pre-formed wishes, in which we form new anticipations of the future based on these partial misinterpretations, in which we are required to reform our interpretations and anticipations, and so on. Religious beliefs which have the stamp of reality are, on this view, beliefs which facilitate this constant correction of personal wish-fantasies by the impact of the unchangeable necessities of life. Religious beliefs which are unreal are beliefs which encourage misinterpretations of reality in accord with personal desires, building up a system that effectively insulates one from the impact of the unchangeable necessities of life.

If religious life is to be understood as a process of growth through the continual interaction of reality and expectation, of revelation and response, and if religious beliefs which have the stamp of reality are those which facilitate this response while unreal beliefs are those which insulate one in a protective covering, then it would seem to follow that real religious thinking must be what the scientists call open-ended thinking, that is, thinking which always has arms open to welcome new truth even when it seems to undermine established truths. It does sometimes happen that a scientist will leap for joy when some other scientist discovers new evidence, even if it upsets his own established theories. It does not often happen that a theologian leaps for joy when some other theologian upsets his theology. Does this mean that a scientist tends to be open-ended in his thinking, while a theologian works within a closed system? Do religions differ in this matter? What is the relation of open-ended thinking to religious claims of finality and uniqueness?

This point is so important it cannot be passed by. The claims to finality and uniqueness, on the one hand, and to openmindedness on the other, are bound to be in the forefront of any encounter between religions. It is significant that both neo-Buddhism and neo-Hinduism make their claims to the allegiance of modern man partly on the ground that their thinking is open-ended and therefore scientific—not on the ground that the conclusions they have reached are scientifically acceptable, but on the ground that the attitude of mind with which they approach the problem of finding solutions is scientifically acceptable.

This is a formidable claim. In order to consider it intelligently we will have to probe a little more deeply into the question of the claims to finality and to open-endedness in thinking. The attitude of the scientist himself gives us a useful starting point. The thinking of the true scientist, we have said, is open-ended in the sense that he welcomes the discovery of new evidence, even when it undermines established theories. But there is one thing about which the thinking of the scientist is not open-ended, that is about the rules of scientific evidence themselves. These are final. Because these are accepted as final he can be open about other things. Finality in one aspect of thinking, and open-endedness in others, seem to belong together as inseparable parts of the total thinking process.

17

When one looks at other areas of experience with this inter-dependence of finality and open-endedness in mind, one begins to find the same pattern reflected everywhere. It is because the phonetic elements of speech are relatively fixed that the immense variability of speech is possible. It is because the alphabet is fixed that the immense variability of literature is possible. It is because the laws of logic are fixed that the immense range of philosophical argument is possible. It is because the love a man and woman have for each other is for them unique and final that each day of life together is an open-ended adventure. It is because each personality is unique and final, corresponding to no fixed stereotype, that its development is an open-ended process whose future is never wholly pre-dictable.

Instead of treating finality and open-mindedness as alterna-tives, therefore, and trying to assign different religions to one camp or the other, it would be better to recognize that each religion claims a measure of finality in some sphere, and is open-ended in some other sphere. The task, then, is to deter-mine which are the areas of finality and of openness in each religion, and to compare them with each other in these terms. The comparison can be illuminating. One might say that early Buddhism claimed finality for its understanding of the nature and cause of human suffering, but was completely open in its thought of God. One might find that Zen Buddhism claimed finality for its understanding of the nature of *satori,* but was open on its views of life beyond death. One might find that Islam claimed finality for the revelation in the Qur'an, but was open about beliefs and practices not rooted in the Qur'an. As for Christianity, one could hardly suggest an area in which it claimed finality and uniqueness better than by retelling a story told of the Indian saint, Sadhu Sundar Singh. It is said that when travelling by train, he was once engaged in discussion by some learned Brahmin fellow-travellers. "Tell us," they said, "what belief you have in Christianity that is not found in Hindu-ism." To which Sadhu Sundar Singh replied: "I have Christ."

And though they reiterated their request, over and over again, he refused to be moved from his simple answer: "I have Christ." As Sadhu Sundar Singh put it, the thing which is final and unique in Christianity is a person, the Word made flesh; while on theological matters the history of the Church shows evidence of a wide range of freedom.

There is one further point one must keep in mind in connection with this matter of finality and openness. The kind of finality that is claimed can have a good deal to do with both the kind and the degree of open-ended thinking that is permitted. The claim to finality can be attached to the conclusion of a process of thinking, that is to a philosophical theory or a theological formulation. When this happens, it tends to put a closure on further open-ended thinking. On the other hand the claim to finality can be attached to something which lies rather at the beginning of a process of thinking than at the end—to something which provides the foundation on which the thinking builds. When this happens, finality releases the mind into a freedom of open thought which is limited only by the necessity of remaining true to its foundation. St. Paul speaks of the glorious liberty of the children of God. For him, the unique and final thing is the event with which the Christian starts, and which creates the possibility of open-ended thinking for him. John Bunyan, with a singularly sensitive insight, placed the decisive event, which made his pilgrim leap three times for joy, near the beginning of his pilgrimage. Everything that followed was an adventure where each day brought new things.

When studying world religions, one is bound to raise questions about the relations of finality and openness in their thought, just as one is bound to ask questions about their factual accuracy, their logical consistency, and their reality. But to be done effectively, such questions must be asked and answered in the dialectic of a conversation.

And so we come back to the point with which we started: the real importance of an open encounter between representatives of world faiths, and of the spirit in which it must take place. Such an encounter must be in the form of a continuing conversation. It must use words. But words create their own problems.

We are accustomed to think of speech as a means of expressing what we think and feel. It can equally be a means of hiding what we think and feel. Studies of interviewing and counselling have shown that people often do use speech in an ambivalent way, both to point to something and to hide its real nature. They are like people who are quite willing to tell a doctor the general area in which trouble is located, but who turn and twist and do everything possible to stop his probing when he begins to touch a really sensitive spot. Words can be used in much the same way. We are quite happy to use them to open up discussion of a problem in a general way; but when the discussion begins to prob too deeply into a problem about which we feel defensive, or a particular belief which we hold specially dear, we can equally well use words to keep discussion away from the sensitive point, on a safe general level. Our conversation is often rather like a wayside sign which says in large letters that anyone can see, "Point of Interest," but adds in small letters below, visible only to those who draw close, "Danger, do not come nearer."

In an encounter between religions, this kind of discussion is disastrous. We must be most careful to guard against it. Fortunately, a good deal is known about the signs of a wrong use of language, and of the conditions which encourage a proper use of language in dialogue.

One of these has already been mentioned. Speech must not be used defensively. The signs of its defensive use are not hard to recognize. There is the habit of avoiding specific issues, and always bringing discussion back to generalities. There is the hair-trigger reaction, the tendency to jump to the defence of something before really thinking what one is saying. There is the recourse to specious rationalizations rather than to specific reasons. There is the tendency to turn a conversation into an ration. There is the quick sense of resentment against questioning or disagreement. It is fairly easy to recognize these in others; the problem is to learn how first to cast the beam out of our own eyes before castigating the conversational mote in our brother's eye. Rigorous self-discipline in eliminating defensive speech from one's own practice is a first essential if effective inter-religious conversations are to develop.

In the second place, the conversation must be what is technically called "permissive." It is important to understand what this means. It does not mean that one should sanction things he believes to be wrong. It does not mean, for instance, that the Muslim should condone idol worship, or that the Buddhist should condone ambition, or that the Christian should condone hatred, or that the Hindu should condone the refusal to condone anything. It does not mean that one should agree to do nothing about practices one believes to be wrong, or doctrines one believes to be false. The whole purpose of initiating conversations is to do something about them, but to do it in a way that will involve, eventually, the active participation of the other party. In a sense, permissiveness simply means refusing to prejudge a case before the other party has had a chance to present it. It means that each party must have a chance to present his case freely, without fear of intimidation or persecution. It assures the other person the same rights one claims for oneself. It means, further, that by one's attitude in conversation, the other person knows he has these rights, and knows he can present his statement honestly without being driven into defensive attitudes.

In the third place, the conversation must be "honest." In trying to understand the meaning of this term we may well run into problems. Anyone can claim to be honest. The real question is as to what he is being honest about. Unfortunately the claim to be honest is frequently used as a cover for a rather insidious form of self-indulgence. One can get a quick insight into how this happens if one recalls how rarely a person claims to be honest when saying something affectionate, pleasant or creditable, and how frequently one claims to be honest when expressing resentment, condemnation or dislike. "I think he's a liar, and I don't care who knows it; at least I'm honest about it," is the kind of thing one may say; or "I think it was a dirty trick to play, and I'm honest enough to say it, let the chips fall where they may." It is worth taking these statements apart to see what they really do say. There is first the explicit statement that someone is a liar or has played a dirty trick. About this we are being quite honest. But there is secondly the statement, at least implicity, that we do not really care about other people, and how our relations with them may be affected by the statement. About this we are being simply dishonest. We do care, greatly. The pretence that we do not care is a sort of bravado to cover temporary resentment or irritation. We are in fact being honest in one part of the statement, and dishonest in another.

This mixture of honesty and dishonesty will not do in a counselling situation, and it will not do in any dialogue of religions. Being honest in the counselling situation means being honest about one's opinions, but in the such a way that it creates neither antagonism nor resentment. It also means being honest about one's real interest in the other person, but in such a way that they will not be led to suppose you will support everything they do or say. And it means being honest in both these ways at the same time. It means being honest, at the same time, both about one's own attitudes, and also about one's recognition of the other person's right to make his own decisions. This kind of honesty is a rare and a difficult thing. But nothing less than this will do in a dialogue of religions. To revert to theological terms, it requires a combination of truth and grace.

Where this kind of conversation can occur between representatives of the world's great religions, the encounter can be anticipiated hopefully. Into this kind of encounter the Christian should be able to enter whole-heartedly. For it was in Christ, claimed the writer of the Gospel of John, that grace and truth came together.

P. NAGARAJA RAO
II. HINDUISM
(The Advaita View as Expounded by Sankara)

In the process of evolution through the ages the emergence of man marks a definite and unique stage. In his composition— physical and biological, he shares the same material with his ancestors—the animals. In the words of Dr. McDougal, "Nature has not constructed man out of any special material which it has not made use of again and again in the composition of the less exalted creatures called animals."[1] In the disposition of man, there are again the same instincts, urges, drives and emotions as in animals. Yet, man is acclaimed as the crown of all creation. In the language of the Holy Bible, "Man is made in the image of God." In the *Aitareya āranyaka,* we have all the distinguishing characteristics of man enumerated. "The spirit is expanded in man. He indeed is most endowed with intelligence, he gives expression to what is known. He knows what is to come. He knows the visible and the invisible worlds. He perceives the immortal through the mortal. Thus is he endowed."[2]

The human being, among all the evolutes of nature, is unique. He has the power of reasoning, the faculty of imagination, to "look before and after and pine for what is not," the gift of speech, the capacity to dream and above all, the free-will to clothe his dreams with reality. He is not a mere physical object or a perishing organism that can be positively or negatively conditioned. He is not a mere creature but is also a creator. By the sheer virtue of the possession of his free-will, man is able to rise above his physical limitations, psychological confines, economic pressure and social oppression. Man has a third dimension to his personality, in addition to the two—the

[1] McDougal, *An Outline of Psychology,* (London: Methuen), p. 134.
[2] *Aiterya āranyaka,* 11. iii. 2.

23

physical and the intellectual. He is something more than a cunning, intellectual biped,[3] for, he has in himself a value-sense

> Oh wearisome condition of Humanity
> Born under one law to another bound
> Vainly begot and yet forbidden vanity
> Created sick commanded to be sound
> What meaneth Nature by these diverse laws
> Passion and Reason self divisions cause.
>
> See Pascal, *Pensées*, 434.

He is self-conscious. He can abstract himself from the event that involve him. He delivers value-judgments, condemns cer tain acts and commends others, he upholds great ideals in the face of grave opposition and danger. He is prepared to drink th cup of hemlock, mount the cross, or face the bullet if it need be in the service of the cause he espouses. In the words of Wal Whitman he alone lies awake in the dark and weeps for his sin and expresses regrets for his wrong acts.[4]

India's great philosopher Sankara clinches the issue in hi commentary on a passage in the *Taittirīya Upanishad*. He ask the question, "In what does the pre-eminence of man consist?" He answers, "It lies in his free-will and knowledge (jñāna karmādhikarāt)".[5] Sankara proclaims the dignity and divinit of man. The Hindu thinkers do not believe that the human bein is the mere combination of the intellect and the body. The discern in the nature of man two other dimensions (in additio to the physical and intellectual), the *moral and spiritual*. It i the spiritual essence in man that enables him to transcend hi physical and intellectual bounds. The Greeks declared "tha man is a rational, a social and a political animal."[6] This defini

---

[3]See Shakespeare's *Hamlet*, Act II, Scene ii, and also Fulke Greville lines—

[4]Walt Whitman describes an animal's life and contrasts it with man's "They are so placid and self-contained, they do not sweat and whine abou their condition, they do not lie awake in the dark and weep for their sins they do not make me sick discussing their duty to God, not one is de mented with the mania of owning things, not one kneels to another, nor t his kind that lived thousands of years ago, not one is respectable or un happy over the whole earth."

[5]*Taittirīya Upanishad*, II, I, i.

[6]Socrates, Plato and Aristotle.

24

tion, to the Hindus leaves out the deepest in man. That is the spiritual in Man. Man is potentially the Spirit.[7]

The Indian genius has largely given its life to two interests: one in finding the meaning and the purpose of life and secondly in outlining an elaborate moral and spiritual discipline for realizing the ideal. Human life is invested, by Hindu thinkers, with great significance. It is not viewed as a mere biological process, destined to end in extinction. Death is not the end of life. Human life is treated as the precious period of probation, challenging the best in man, and affording him an opportunity to grow to his best. The world is not a wasteland nor is human life a gladiatorial show or a perplexity. It is not a puzzle nor an enigma nor a mere welter of events governed by chance, leading to no definite known or knowable ends. Nor is life to be considered an amusement park for men to live a life of unbridled passions. Life is described by Dr. Radhakrishnan as "a succession of spiritual opportunities."[8]

Life is the gift of nature. Intelligent living and the wise ordering of our emotions are the result of strenuous ethical efforts and spiritual wisdom. The great Hindu scripture Gītā asks us to cherish "a reverence for life." Human life is so ordered as to enable man to distinguish the transient from the eternal, the pleasant from the good, and the noble from the ignoble. In one sense, the Hindus accept the verdict of the philosopher Leibniz, that this is the best of all possible worlds.

Human experience and reflective meditation shake man from his stupour. He wants to find the aim of existence and the meaning of life. The meaning of life for man is to realize his full and immense potentialities and bring them out, in his moral and spiritual life.

The living religion of the Hindus is the Vedānta philosophy. The Vedānta is the general name describing the group of philosophical systems that seek to systematize in a consistent manner

---

[7] *Atma brahma ca.*

[8] S. Radhakrishnan, *An Idealist View of Life,* (New York: Barnes & Noble), chapter vii.

the message of the triple texts—the *Upanishads,* the *Gītā* and the *Brahmasūtras.* There are two prominent schools of Vedānta, both rival schools. They strive hard to establish that their system is the one entrenched in the triple texts. The rival schools are the Idealistic Monism of Sankara and the Theistic Personalism of Ramanuja. Both these schools have interpreted the meaning of life in different ways. Let us advert to the consideration of the meaning of life and the aim of existence as laid down in the philosophy of Sankara called Advaita. The fundamental concept of Sankara's system of philosophy is that ultimate Reality is the non-dual Spirit. The Absolute Spirit is unconditioned existence and unexcellable bliss. Man in his essence is non-different from the Absolute Spirit—Brahman Sankara proclaims "the great equation" of the Absolute Spirit with man, on the basis of his spiritual experience, scriptural declaration and reasoning.

The unregenerate human being in his empirical life is oblivious to the consubstantiality of man and the Absolute. His ignorance of the identity makes him feel that he is a mortal being, "given away to misery and mortality, tortured in life and swallowed up in death." Man imagines that he is made in vain. Many are confused about the mystery of life; they externalize in their philosophies their own autobiography. To some, "who are born to endless pain," life is just meanness and mechanism. Some find, as Hardy does, that joy is only an episode in the universal drama of pain—called the human life.[9] Yet others regard man as a pleasure-seeking animal. They advise him to respond to the call of Hedonism, "to eat, to drink and to be merry in a variety of ways ere we die." These men in the words of the poet are busy getting and spending—they lay waste their powers. They take to the pleasures of life avidly. They do not vex their souls with impossible longings. They do not look before and after, nor do they debate about fate or free-will. They live

---

[9]Thomas Hardy, *Mayor of Casterbridge,* (New York: New American Library). Last sentence.

happy lives with untroubled minds and uninhibited emotions.[10] They are intellectually smart, quick to question, ready to disbelieve and they hold that nothing matters. The cynics among them broadcast the scientific truth that death is the end of man. Death is sure to lay us all flat alike, we are passing shadows, creatures of the moment. Life is insignificant and death is without any consequence. Failure is unimportant and success is meaningless. This school is the Nihilism of the modern intellectual.

Experience and logic point to the error and the defect in the theories that confine ultimate Reality and the essence of man only to the level of the senses. Hedonism and secularism are only theories of the first look and not the products of deep logical thought. Man has a self, deeper than his senses and mind. Sense-pleasures are conditioned and short-lived. They are mediated and are subject to the law of diminution. Continued indulgence in sense pleasures leaves man utterly worn out with "remorse of conscience" and the "dissipation of the spirit." The deeper self in man is not satisfied with the sum of the successive varied satisfactions.[11] The spirit in man is not satisfied with physical fulfilment or intellectual excitement. The Spirit in man seeks to make life a perfect instrument and vehicle for the purpose of realizing the immense potentialities of man. The realization of the true nature of the self is the destiny of man, the aim of existence and the purpose of life. Sankara anticipates Hermann Hess's celebrated declaration—there is only one true vocation for everyone, "to seek one's self."

According to the Absolutist persuasion, expounded by Sankara in his philosophy, the average unregenerate man is totally oblivious to his potential nature in his empirical existence. He

[10]See Llewellyn Powes, *Glory of Life*. The Indian materialist exhorts

> "While life is yours, live joyously
> None can escape death's searching eye
> When once this frame of ours they burn
> How shall it ever again return?"

See S. Radhakrishnan, *Recovery of Faith*, pp. 91-103.

[11]See *Manu smrti*, II. 94.

is unaware of the unity of the Spirit and existence. He does not know that ultimate Reality is one infinite Spirit which appears in empirical life as the world of matter and the group of individuals. Sankara explains the relation between many and the One in an unique manner. The Spirit does not create directly the things of the world. Nor are the things of the world and souls the transformations of ultimate Reality. Relation between the spirit and the world of souls is the relation of Appearance to Reality. It is a one-sided theory of causation (vivarta). There is nothing besides the Spirit real. Outside the Spirit everything is unreal. The Spirit is in no way affected by the blemishes and the taints present in empirical existence. The world-appearance is dependent on the Spirit. The effect is dependent on the cause. The reverse is not true.[12] To clinch the issue, there is no organic connection between the Absolute Spirit and the world of Appearance. The stock example employed to illustrate this relation is the delusive perception of the rope as the snake in twilight, the mistaking of the mother-of-pearl for silver.

According to Sankara, besides Brahman—the Absolute Spirit—there is another principle which though not eternal is still beginning less operative in life. This is the transcendental illusion—the celebrated theory of Maya. The one, second-less, real, eternal Spirit appears as the many. The power of māyā hides the real—does not stop there, but also shows up an unreal projection in its place. It conceals the object and superimposes something else in its place. In twilight, we do not see the rope and in its place, we apprehend a snake. The same principle, māyā, conceals the true nature of Brahman, the Spirit, which is infinite Bliss, Knowledge and Existence (Sat-cit-ānanda) and projects in its place the indescribable, variegated, manifold souls and things. When, this world-appearance began, we cannot say Why it did so, we cannot answer.

It may be contended, that the phenomena of world-appearance is not intelligible. It is difficult for us to believe how the one, infinite, Spirit is mistaken for the Tom, Dick and Harry

[12]Sankara, commentary on *Vedanta Sutras*. II. i. 14.

men who are full of ignorance and experiencing alternate moods of pleasure and pain. Sankara's answer to the question is—Look in, and analyze your experience. The transcendental illusion—māyā—is the experience of all of us. We identify the body with our Self. We say, we are blind and deaf, when our sense-organs are affected. We say, " I am stout," "I am happy," "I am unhappy," when our body experiences such feelings. We constantly mistake the Spirit for the body, the mind and the senses.[13] The very texture of our experience is supported by this identification. Such an identification of the not-self in the self is the pre-condition of all experience. As long as we have this experience, we will feel that we are all competing, conflicting centres of life. Plurality of Selves persists as long as we live in the world of māyā. We are like the men in the cave of Plato's Republic,[14] who can only see the shadows and are confined to the world of shadows in the cave. It is only the philosophers of Plato who can contemplate the Sun in all its splendour and can perceive reality.

The high-destiny of man, according to Sankara, is the call to break this pluralist-illusion and realize the unitive experience. The spirit is the self in all. It is one and not many (ātma sarvasya, ātma).

The paradox of man is, he is infinite. That is why he knows his finite limitations and chafes under it. The Infinite in him and that he is, struggles to realize Itself. We have perceptions and intimations of the unitive experience in the significant moments of our artistic and aesthetic experience. We feel that we are eternal and not banished strangers, tied down to the body of lust, without a glimmer of divinity. It is the realization of the unitive experience that unwraps the several thick sheaths that cover and hide the true nature of man. To unveil the deepest layer and to get into contact with the spirit, which is the essence of man, is summed up in the exhortation—know thyself (ātmanam viddhi).

---

[13]Sankara on *Vedanta Sutras*. See Preface ix. *adyasa bhasya*.
[14]Plato's *Republic*, Book VII.

It is such an experience alone that can transform man and "convert his plodding mentality into spiritual illumination." Sankara regards such an experience as the birthright of all individuals. It is not a production of what is not there. It is realizing what is already real. Sankara finds bold confirmation for his daring speculative findings in the unfaltering affirmations of the Upanisads, in their majestic and epigrammatic utterances, which are designated as the great sayings—That Thou Art (tat tvam asi) ; I am Brahma (aham brahmasmi) ; The self is Brahman (ātmā ca brahma).

Human life presents the tragic spectacle of "maddening monstrous contrasts" and cruel competition in its pluralist phase. The sovereign remedy for the malady is the realization of the unity of existence. It is only spiritual experience that can inspire selflessness in man. At the end of his Indian tour, Paul Deussen said to a gathering at Bombay, "The Gospels quite correctly establish as the highest law of morality, 'Love your neighbour as yourself.' But why should I do so, since by the order of nature, I feel pain and pleasure only in myself, not in my neighbour?" He asserts that, the answer is not in the Holy Bible, but in the Vedānta of Sankara, in the great formula 'That Thou Art,' which gives in three words the combined sum of metaphysics and morals. "You shall love your neighbour as yourself, because, you are in essence non-different from your neighbour." The genuine, immediate, self-certifying experience of the oneness of all alone can make for genuine Humanism. Otherwise, secular humanism, benevolent altruism, consideration for others are only based on good manners and have no roots in man to make them enduring. Spiritual experience alone can make for universalism.

The Absolution of Sankara is criticized on many counts. The pluralists of our age, who cherish the value of individuality are shocked at the destruction of the same in Brahman realization. They argue that such a view belittles individuality and promotes a disgust for life and slackens human effort. The moment we discount individuality, the reverence for life dwindles.

Sankara and his followers take up this challenge. They highlight the distinction between individuality and personality. According to Sankara, the finite individual has a limited intelligence and his outlook is monstrously constricted. Such a truncated nature of man, cannot be described as his personality. The true personality of man is spiritual nature. Viewed in this light, spiritual experience does not destroy anything of permanent value. It only enables the human being to shed his limitations. Such a prospect is not without attractions for man. For, it is in man not to be satisfied till he reaches his highest stature. This attractive goal eggs him on to lead a life of selfless altruism.

To realize the one-ness of all is not easy for man. Nature and biological instincts perpetuate man's bondage. Spinoza observes "Submission to passion is bondage; exercise of reason is freedom." For realizing the spirit, one has to reverse the current of biological drives and run counter to it. Strenuous ethical effort, perseverance of the goal and unremitting toil are necessary for this realization.

"Reverence for life"—a phrase given currency by Schweitzer—has a place in Sankara's philosophy. Spiritual realization, the destiny of man and the goal of human life is not to be achieved only after death. It can be realized here and now in this very physical frame of ours. Such a realization is called *"jivanmukti."*[15] Self-realization is not the production of something new, which is not already there. The Upanishads declare that to be oblivious of this high destiny is to sustain a great loss. "If one realizes Brahman here, that is the great truth. If one fails to realize It here, great is the loss."[16] If we fail to realize the true nature of ourself, life would be merely "a tale told by an idiot, full of sound and fury, signifying nothing." Human life, affords us opportunities to overcome the pluralistic outlook. The Hindu mind realizes that one life is too short for man to overcome the illusion that we are discrete separate entities. It is the experience of the unitive nature of the Spirit that makes us

---

[15]*Bhagavad Gita,* V, 19.
[16]*Kena Upanishad,* II, 5.

aware of the mutual involvement of all. Gandhi pinpointed this truth in his utterance. "There cannot be happiness for any of us, until it is won for all." The indivisibility of humanity and its integral nature are experienced in Brahman realization. Sankara, in one of his minor poetical works refers to birth as a human being, as the greatest of the blessings for man.[17]

Spiritual realization is the birthright of all. This follows from the metaphysics of Sankara. Realization is merely the negation of our finitude. Sankara declared often that only Brahman realization can help us to overcome the conflicts, tensions, doubt and strife in our hearts. The road to spiritual realization is through morality. None can bypass it. The Katha Upanishad declares, "The man who has not turned away from his evil ways, who is not tranquil, who has no concentration of mind and whose mind is not at rest, cannot realize the Self, through mere knowledge."[18]

The moral life is not the same as the spiritual life. Morality implies duality. At the moral level, the individual is aware of both the sides of the question, the pros and cons of a problem. He chooses the good after some deliberation and strife, even against the pull of his pleasure-instinct. In contrast, at the spiritual level, the individual transcends this duality and is spontaneously virtuous. He does not "realize virtue but reveals it." His work is worship, his conduct is consecration and his words are wisdom. This is the fruit of the Spirit. He experiences a peace which passeth all understanding. It is only spiritual realization that can enable an individual to practise "charity," in the Christian sense of the term, as described by St. Paul. Spiritual experience spells fearlessness. It is only the individual souls, anchored in the spirit that work for the welfare of the world. They are the salt of the earth. They bring light into the world of darkness. Life itself presents a new picture, after the experience. We see the glory of the Spirit in all. We are no longer teased about the meaning of life, nor

---

[17]*Viveka cūdāmani*, v. 2.
[18]*Katha Upanishad*, I, ii, 24.

confused about the aim of existence, or unaware of the purpose of the universe.

When we describe spiritual experience as the ultimate test of religion, Sankara escapes, by doing so, the charge of dogmatism. Scripture posits the existence of the oneness of ultimate Reality, reason explains Its possibility, experience proves Its truth on our pulse. The direct intuition of the Absolute is religious experience. The Upanishads blazen forth "The self cannot be realized by scriptures nor by intellectual probity, nor by the astuteness of the intellect. It can only be realized by him, who chooses it."[19] It is this experience that is at the basis of universal love. "We should do unto others, as we do to ourselves, because they are ourselves—a view which places the golden rule of morality on the surest of foundations."

When one talks of the meaning of life, the natural question about the place of reason in life arises before us for our consideration. Reason is not denied a legitimate place. One should not be an arrogant free-thinker nor a blind literalist. The spiritual aspirant after acquiring moral competence should seek spiritual instruction from a competent teacher, from a study of the scriptures. This is called s'ravana. Reason steps in to examine the pros and cons of the teaching and assimilates it. Reflection removes the doubts that assail the mind. Reason does not discover the truth, it demonstrates it, when intuition discloses it. Reason establishes the probability of scriptural truths. Spiritual experience demonstrates it.[20] Sankara observes, "What is accepted or believed in, without thorough inquiry prevents one from reaching the goal, and results in great evil."[21] On another occasion he remarks "that a hundred scriptural statements cannot turn a pot into a cloth." Reasoning is good, and the perverse use of it is condemned. Sankara was not slow to discern the limitations of reasoning. He points out that its findings are non-conclusive and surpassed. Reasoning cannot

[19]*Ibid.*, I, ii. 23.
[20]Sankara on *Vedanta sutras*.
[21]*Ibid.*, I. i. 1.

prescribe the ends or goals of life. Reasoning at best, is an instrument. Reasoning, as Tagore puts it, is "all blade and no handle." It can be pressed into service for any cause. Reasoning which does not run counter to scriptural truths is to be accepted.

Another important criticism against the philosophy of Sankara is, that he regards the world as illusory. Such a criticism arises from a crude understanding and a cruel interpretation of the māyā doctrine. Sankara declares the world as māyā, he does not compare it to dreams. The world of waking —experience is distinguished from dream. Dream-experience is private to each individual. On waking, the dreams are sublated. The universe is not a dream. It is objective and not a subjective fancy, nor a private dream. There is a common reference to it by all. The world lasts till we have Brahman experience. All our moral and spiritual efforts, we undertake in the world of waking-experience. The individual does not create the world. He has to accept it. Hence, it is wrong to regard the world as illusory. Dr. Radhakrishnan has summed up the position—"unreal the world is, illusory it is not."

Sankara clearly distinguishes three levels of reality. One, the transcendental level where Spirit alone is Reality. Second, the empirical level where the world persists, and we have plurality of souls. In between them, we have the dream-world. The empirical world is not a dream, neither a delirium nor a fantasy.

Sankara was no Subjective Idealist nor a Solipsist. He upheld different degrees of reality and levels of experience. Sankara never reduced the world to a welter of ideas. It is wrong to state and unfair to describe Sankara's philosophy as illusory.

Some of the opponents to the philosophy of Sankara feel that he does not make an adequate provision for the concept of God. The Absolute of Sankara is described as indeterminate and is without any attributes. Besides the Absolute, Sankara

34

posits the conditioned aspect of the Absolute. The God of Sankara is not a second entity different from the Absolute. God is the Absolute in the context of the world. He is not on the same level as the individual soul. Sankara's God called Iswara is in possession of māyā and is not delimited by it as the individual soul. Sankara's God projects, by his power, the world of pots and pans with all its entrancing variety, which even baffles imagination. Advaita tradition traces world-appearance to God's power. The spiritual aspirant cannot bypass God. He has to worship Him and then transcend the conception. Professors Datta and Chatterjee have summarized the issue in their excellent manual on Indian Philosophy. "Sankara is sometimes accused of atheism. This charge falls or stands according as God is taken . . . If God connotes among other things supreme Reality, Sankara's theory is not surely atheism, but the logical perfection of the theistic faith. Indeed, whereas atheism believes only in the world and not in God, and ordinary theism believes in both, the world and God, Sankara believes only in God. For him, God is the only Reality. Rather than denying God, he makes most of God . . . If this type of faith is to be distinguished from ordinary theism, the word for it should be, not atheism but rather *super-theism.*"[22]

Sankara's concept of the Absolute is not a blank nothing. Pure being is not non-being.[23] Any conception of ultimate Reality, which we try to bring into the conspectus of discussive reason is imperfect. Sankara is anxious to remove all possible traces of anthropomorphism in his conception of the Absolute. The human qualities, even the most glorious and highest of them are pitifully inadequate. They militate against the perfection and infinity of the Absolute. Sankara's Absolute is a powerful and drastic corrective to the sentimental and anthropomorphic conception of God.

---

[22]S. Chatterjee and D. M. Datta, *An Introduction to Indian Philosophy,* (Calcutta University: Luzac), p. 395.

[23]Hegel in the west, and the nyaya school, India, held the view "that pure-being is non-being."

The Absolute of philosophy is described as the God of religion, in the relational context. There are no two Brahmans in Advaita. The one, Brahman is presented under two aspects —the Absolute and God. Bradley's God falls short of the Absolute and hence is distressing to the religious consciousness of man. In a memorable sentence, Bradley sums up the issue. "Short of the Absolute, God cannot rest and having reached that goal, He is lost and religion with Him."[24] Such a contingency does not arise in the case of Sankara. Those of us in India who have seen the institutional and organizational practices and traditions of religion established by Sankara in different mathes of India, can testify to the high place accorded to God by Sankara. The devotional hymns of Sankara are marvels of poetry and condensations of his metaphysics. They are alike literary masterpieces and metaphysical manuals. The poetry is soul-stirring. The language is musical. Sankara's philosophy permits the liberty to the aspirant to view and worship the Absolute under any aspect. Once the Absolute is described as indeterminate, there is no dogmatizing about It. It escapes all limitations of a clearly-defined anthropomorphic conception. Sankara has no quarrel with the followers of other religions. His broad-based concept of the Absolute permits any description of It. All descriptions are equally true and none of them is exhaustive of the Absolute. The Rgveda declared—"Reality is one and wise men call It by various names and approach It by many paths."[25] The differences in the temperament of men, account for the plurality of approaches and alternate standpoints.[26] Symmachus, in his controversy with St. Ambrose, observed "The heart of so great a mystery cannot be reached by following one road only." The meaning of life for Sankara is the realization of the unity of existence and translation of it into one's life.

[24]F. H. Bradley, *Appearance and Reality,* (Oxford U.P.), p. 398.
[25]*Rgveda.*
[26]*Bhagavad Gita,* IV.

SHOYU HANAYAMA

III. BUDDHISM

PREFACE

Buddhists often chant a passage of reliance on the three treasures of Buddhism: the Buddha, the Dharma and the Sangha. This is a shortened form of this passage which reads as follows:

How fortunate I was to be born a human being! It is the hardest of the hardest things to be born a human being. Again how fortunate I was to be given a chance to know Buddhism! It is also very seldom that one is given a chance to know it. Therefore, if I could not attain enlightenment in this present life, I would not ever be able to attain the enlightenment. Realizing this, I, together with the masses who also realized it, sincerely rely upon the three holy treasures of Buddhism: the Buddha (the Enlightened One), the Dharma (Truth) and the Sangha (Group of Priests who pursue the Dharma).

Buddhism starts with the realization of the difficulty to be born a human being. To be born a human being among innumerable living beings on this earth is surely the hardest of the hardest things. Then how is it that I could be born a human being in this present world? The answer to this question from a Buddhist standpoint will be given below.

There will be as many ways to live in present day society as there are people. There are many people who live in suffering and agony throughout their lives. On the other hand, it seems that there are some people who live happily without any material and spiritual dissatisfaction throughout their lives. Again there are not a few who pass away due to illness and other reasons when they are only small babies or children. There also are many people who are able to enjoy long lives. For such, it is easy to answer the question: Which one of them is happier? However, is it real happiness simply to live long? or is it possible to live a happy life without any material dissatisfactions?

In speaking of the meaning and purpose of life according to the Buddhist interpretation, it will be necessary to make clear what we Buddhists regard as real happiness in this life.

Generally speaking, wealth, property, status, prestige, longevity, to have a suitable spouse, and to have lovely children are regarded as factors or elements in living happily in this life. Many people believe that the meaning and purpose of life to live happily is attained in getting these factors and elements in this life. And to some extent this is true because nobody can deny the fact that these constitute certainly some reasons why people live happily in this world. We are not able to live without such things as food, clothes, and houses. However, we know that there are not a few people who are unhappy in spite of the fact that they possess all of these factors which help one to live happily.

What then do we have to do to pursue real happiness in this life? If we can make this clear, then we will be able to show the meaning and purpose of life. In order to clarify the way by which Buddhists enjoy real happiness, I would like to start with the reason why Sakyamuni Buddha, the founder of Buddhism, abandoned his apparently happy life and entered into the life of a wanderer in search of Truth.

THE LIFE OF SAKYAMUNI BUDDHA

What was the reason for Sakyamuni abandoning everything in his worldly life, which objectively seemed to be so happy, and beginning to observe hard ascetic practices and engaging in meditation? If we can clarify this point, then we shall be able to understand clearly the meaning and purpose of life from the Buddhist standpoint.

Sakyamuni was born about the middle of the sixth century B.C. as the Crown Prince of the King Suddhodana, the ruler of the Sakya clan in the northern part of India. Rejoicing over the birth of the heir, the King made elaborate arrangements to see that nothing was lacking in the life of the young Prince. Therefore, it can be easily imagined that Sakyamuni was brought up under circumstances in which no material dissatisfaction was experienced. When he was only nineteen years of age, he married a beautiful girl, Yasodhara, a princess of the neighbouring Kingdom, and a boy was born to them. In all objective senses, it cannot be considered that his everyday life as the prince was unhappy. If he would continue his lay-life, he would succeed his father and would become the king. However, at twenty-nine years of age, he abandoned all that he had, as well as his beloved wife and son, and entered into the life of seclusion and asceticism.

Immediately after his birth, Sakyamuni's mother had passed away and he had been brought up by his aunt. The fact that his mother had passed away, however, cannot be considered as the direct reason for his entrance to the priesthood, because that had occurred when he was only a small baby.

According to Buddhist tradition, it is believed that he realized the impermanence of this world on the occasion of his seeing an old man, a sick person and a corpse. Then when he saw a priest he made up his mind to become one in order to discover the way of deliverance from this world which is so full of agony and suffering.

Anyway, it is true that the reason why Sakyamuni abandoned his lay-life, which objectively seemed to be so happy, was his realization of the impermanence of this life.

That is to say, he abandoned his worldly life when he realized the fact that all existences and phenomena of this world are but temporal and impermanent, and that all those who are born have to die and all that which exists will become extinguished.

39

When he realized this, he felt that all worldly pleasures and happiness were temporal and he could not continue his life as the prince. Therefore, he became a wanderer seeking truth in order to find the real happiness which must not be temporal for himself and his fellow beings.

Having left the palace and all that he held dear, he first visited some priests of Brahmanism, India's traditional religion, to be taught the way which he wanted to know. But when he realized that the teachings of Brahmanism were not the way which leads to real truth, he left them. Thereafter, he observed hard ascetic practices for six long years, only to abandon them also, when again he found that they were not for him the real way to discover the truth. Finally, however, after he had sat quietly in meditation alone under the Bodhi tree near the Nairanjana river, he attained the state of enlightenment.

That was when he was thirty-five years of age, and it was at that time that he became the Buddha. "Buddha" is a Sanskrit term which has the meaning of "the Enlightened One." What was the Truth or Way which Sakyamuni attained?

FUNDAMENTAL DOCTRINES OF BUDDHISM

Buddhism arose in India about two thousand five hundred years ago under the teaching and inspiring leadership of Sakyamuni Buddha. During the course of many years, it was transmitted to various countries in Asia. On the one hand, it moved north into China and became the object of both serious study and devout practice. But there arose a Chinese Buddhism which was not necessarily the same as the Buddhism in India. Then about the middle of the sixth century of the Christian era, Chinese Buddhism was introduced into Japan via Korea. This type of Buddhism is generally called Mahayana Buddhism, that is, the Buddhism of the Great Vehicle. On the other hand, Buddhism was also transmitted into southeast Asian countries such as Burma, Ceylon, Cambodia, Laos, Thailand and Vietnam. This type of Buddhism is called either Theravada Buddhism, that is the Buddhism of Traditional Teachers, or Hinayana Buddhism, the Buddhism of the Lesser Vehicle. Generally speaking, the former term is preferred by the leaders of this type.

Moreover, in the long course of Buddhist history, various sects and schools arose from each of these two types of Buddhism, but more especially from Mahyana Buddhism. There are many reasons why Buddhism as originally expounded by Sakyamuni Buddha became divided into various kinds of sects and schools. Moreover, we can account for many differences, both in doctrine and ritual services as well as in the practices and precepts, of these various Buddhist sects and schools. Dissimilarity in nationality, time, race, culture, civilization, circumstances, customs, and class have contributed to the diversities of belief and practice.

Nevertheless, so long as they are Buddhist sects and schools, there are many universal doctrines which permeate through all sects and schools in all countries and in all ages. If we can understand these universal doctrines in Buddhism, then it will be easy to know the general idea of Buddhists of all types towards the problem of "the meaning and purpose of life." Therefore, we must now turn our attention to some of the universal and fundamental doctrines of Buddhism.

First of all, we must note that the universal and fundamental doctrines of Buddhism were naturally expounded by Sakyamuni, the founder of Buddhism, but they were not invented by Sakyamuni. They were universal and eternal principles or truths which had existed from time immemorial. It is true that he realized these truths and it was through the realization of these truths that he attained enlightenment. It is also true that he systematized these truths into the form which we call Buddhism and that after him Buddhist doctrines were greatly developed and various profound doctrines were added to and systematized by many great priests of various countries. However, it must be remembered that these truths themselves had been in existence even before the enlightenment of Sakyamuni. What Sakyamuni did was to discover and to attain the Truth and through his own experiences and efforts systematized it into the form of Buddhism.

One of the fundamental or universal doctrines of Buddhism is the concept of Hetu-pratyaya which means "direct and indirect causes" which manifests the mutual relationship of all existences and phenomena of this world, or Pratitya-samutpada which means "dependent origination", which means that all existences and phenomena of this world originate dependently through the chain of causation.

All existences and phenomena of this world are mutually related and nothing can exist independently. In this world, there is not even a single existence or phenomenon which is completely independent or isolated and has no relation with anything else. In order to make this idea of causation clear, a concrete example will be given.

I was born of my parents just as all other human beings. It is true that the direct and the most important cause or factors in my birth were my parents. However, there were innumerable other indirect factors or causes which made it possible for me to be born in this present world. If my father and mother had not married each other, but had married other people, *I* would never have been born. The fact that no other person married mother, for example, is the indirect cause or negative cause for my being born as myself and not someone else. Again, if my grandparents on both my father's side and my mother's side had married any other persons than my grandfathers or grandmothers, then *I* would never have been born. Therefore, it can be said that all the men and women who did not marry my parents or my grandparents or other direct lineal ancestors must surely have some relation to my birth.

How many ancestors does a single individual have a thousand years ago? The number is staggering. Each human being has two parents, a mother and a father, and each of them naturally has two parents. Thus there are eight grandparents for one person. Estimating a single generation as approximately thirty years, then three hundred years ago, there had to be $2 \times 2 \times 2 \times 2 \times 2 \times 2 \times 2 \times 2 \times 2 \times 2$ or 1,024 ancestors for each person. If we were to continue this kind of calculation further back, say for nine hundred years, we would reach the conclusion that each individual must have more than 1,000,000,000 ancestors. But, of course, this is pure mathematical calculation. There are other factors that must be taken into consideration, because it is impossible to think that there were more than 1,000 million people in any country nine hundred years ago. However, through such calculation, it can be easily imagined, on the one hand, that there is not even a single person who is completely without any relation to some person in the past, or on the other hand, that there is not even a single person who has nothing to do with others in the present. Now, we shall be able to conclude that all human beings both in the past and present had and have mutual relations and that their birth is dependent upon the existence of all other human beings. Again we can fully understand that we are chained by innumerable direct and indirect causes of self and others in the past. Such a concept of causation in Buddhism, as you of course recognize, does not contradict the modern scientific spirit.

The same relation or chain of causation can be considered in the case of all other beings and phenomena of this world.

For example, sunshine, fertilizer, water, and earth are all indispensable factors in causing seeds of plants to bud. Without these elements or factors it is impossible for seeds to bud. However, they are not the only causes for seeds to bud. There are innumerable indirect causes which make possible for them to bud. If a bird should come and pick up a seed and eat it up, this seed would never bud. Again, if a man, consciously or unconsciously, should come and crush it, or if heavy rain should fall and make it decay, or a strong wind should blow it off into the water, then this seed would never bud. That no bird ate the seed, that no man crushed it, that no rain made it decay, that no wind carried it off into the water—these are indirect negative causes or factors which enable the seed to bud.

Such a relation among all existences and phenomena of this world is called Hetu-pratyaya. The reason for which all existences can originate and continue to exist is called Pratitya-samutpada. Such origination and relation can be considered as covering all existences and phenomena of this world.

Here, however, we must note that this concept of causation and origination of all existences in Buddhism should never be regarded as a kind of fatalism.

It is true that all our deeds in everyday life are caused by and linked to innumerable direct and indirect causes in the past that are related to ourselves and others. Moreover, at the same time, our deeds in the present become direct and indirect causes of future results related to ourselves and others. When a person realizes the fact that his present deeds will be the indirect cause of future acts related to himself, he cannot but behave in respect to even a single deed in everyday life without the greatest care.

Sometimes, however, due to many indirect causes of which he himself may not be aware, a person may fail even if he should try to do his best. In such cases, we must not consider only the immediate result. Our future will never be fixed by any such acts, because we ourselves are able to make the future through our present deeds as well as our past deeds. Of course, our future is chained by innumerable indirect causes through others, but they are not absolute causes for us.

In connection with such a concept of causation, Sakyamuni expounded the doctrine of the Four Noble Truths. They are (1) the Fact of Suffering, (2) the Cause of Suffering, (3) the Cessation of Suffering, and (4) the Path which leads to the Cessation of Suffering. Sakyamuni emphatically explained that, first of all, we should fully recognize the fact of suffering in all phenomena in this world. That is to say, old age is suffering, illness is suffering, death is suffering, separation from those whom we love is suffering, the presence of those whom we hate is suffering, and not to obtain what we desire is suffering. By realizing this, we shall be able to recognize that even our own birth and existence is suffering. This is the Truth of Suffering, the first of the Four Noble Truths.

Next, we have to understand the reason why there is suffering in the world. We have to realize the Cause of Suffering. The Cause of Suffering is the tormenting craving or thirst for worldly existence and phenomena. Because of our tormenting craving or thirst, all worldly phenomena such as old age, illness, death, meeting those whom we hate, not obtaining what we desire, being separated from those whom we love result in suffering. This is the Truth of the Cause of Suffering, the second of the Four Noble Truths.

When we are able to realize fully the Cause of Suffering, we have to try to stop it. Unless we are able to stop such tormented cravings or thirst for worldly phenomena, we shall not be able to attain the enlightenment in which we can realize the true meaning of life. This is the Truth of the Cessation of Suffering, the third of the Four Noble Truths.

Then how can we remove the Cause of Suffering? In order to be delivered from it, we have to follow the Path which leads to the cessation of this tormenting craving or thirst. This is the Truth of Path, the fourth of the Four Noble Truths. This is the practical path which all Buddhists must follow in order to attain enlightenment. This Truth of Path is the Eightfold Right Path: Right Views (right understanding of the Buddha's teachings), Right Consideration (of the Truth), Right Words (which are true), Right Conduct (in everyday life), Right Way of Life (in society), Right Efforts (to attain the enlightenment), Right Mindfulness (right use of the intellect), and Right Meditation (to enter Buddhahood). Through the practice of this Eightfold Right Path, one shall be able to avoid all sufferings of this world. The supreme goal set before all Buddhists is the escape from suffering, ignorance and desire, and the attainment of the Truth of Enlightenment. Through pursuing this lofty ideal, one can find out the meaning of real happiness for man.

Other fundamental and universal doctrines of Buddhism are the concepts of Sunyata (non-substantiality: this Sanskrit term is usually translated into English as "emptiness" or "nothingness," but, in my belief, such translations are not suitable. Therefore, I would like to use the term "non-substantiality" in this essay—Anitya (impermanence) and Anatman (Selflessness).

All existences and phenomena of this world which originated by innumerable direct and indirect causes are neither substantial nor permanent, but temporal and impermanent existences and phenomena. Namely, nothing exists in this world which is substantial and permanent. Nobody can deny the fact that all those who are born will die and again all things which have been created and originated will be extinguished some day in the future. As I mentioned above, therefore, the concept of Sunyata does not necessarily mean the emptiness or nothingness of existences and phenomena of this world. Through such a concept of non-substantiality of all existences and phenomena, we can see and observe things and phenomena of this world as they are. If we could realize this, we would abandon all attachments and desires to worldly existences which are neither eternal nor substantial, and would begin to search for the truth. In this connection, the existence of the Self or Ego, which is believed in many religions to exist permanently and apart from one's body, is completely denied in Buddhism. In other words, Buddhism is a religion of the Selflessness or Egolessness, because it denies any permanent existence in this world.

Then what will be the meaning and purpose of life in such an impermanent and non-substantial world? Before answering this question, I would like to investigate Buddhist doctrines a little further.

The state in which one attained enlightenment is called Nirvana (perfect tranquility). Originally, Nirvana meant the death of Sakyamuni Buddah. But in later interpretations of Buddhism, this state is understood as the ultimate state which all Buddhists, irrespective of sects and schools, try to attain.

Nirvana is the state in which one can realize the truth and abandon all worldly desires and attachments through the realization of the impermanence and non-substantiality of this world not only by one's mind but also by his body. It cannot be said that he is in the state of Nirvana if one understands Buddhist doctrines only in his mind and does not practise it actually in his life. For example, I, as an individual, can fully understand that this world is impermanent and non-substantial in my mind, but yet I cannot abandon all worldly desires such as money, prestige, property, and other things. Therefore, I am not in the state of Nirvana at present as I cannot realize the concept of impermanence and non-substantiality in this actual life, in spite of the fact that I know and understand all doctrines of Buddhism in my mind. Nirvana does not necessarily mean death. However, in many Buddhist sects and schools, it is believed that Nirvana can be attained only after death, because it will be almost impossible for human beings to abandon all worldly desires and instinctive passions in this present life.

In present Buddhism, this term Nirvana is often used as the synonym for enlightenment, and it is all right to understand that the state of Nirvana is the attainment of enlightenment or Buddhahood.

Besides the above fundamental and universal doctrines of Buddhism, there is one important thought or standpoint in Buddhism. It is the theory of "teachings in accordance with the ability of men."

It will be almost impossible to imagine that there are two persons in this world who are exactly the same in their abilities in all respects. There must be some differences in their abilities even in the case of twins. Therefore, according to Buddhism, it must be admitted that there are as many teachings as there are variations in the abilities of people in this world. In order to clarify such a standpoint of Buddhism, I will show you again some examples.

It will be very tiresome for the students of universities or colleges to be taught some easy problems of mathematics such as two plus two equals four. On the other hand, it will be meaningless for the pupil of elementary schools and middle schools to be taught some problems of differential or integral calculus. However, propositions such as two plus two equals four are also certain truth for students of universities and colleges, even though they seem very simple. However, comprehension and understanding of the same proposition is fairly different in accordance with the ability of men as well as their education, age, circumstances, and physical condition. Therefore, it is not strange that there are various teachings in Buddhism in accordance with the ability of the followers. Again, it is also not strange to say that each of them is a manifestation of the Truth. In order to lead all people who are different in their ability, there must be various teachings. Therefore, there are a great many sutras, treatises, and other texts which are different in their contents and doctrines in Buddhism, all of which are believed to be taught by Sakyamuni Buddha according to the ability of followers.

According to modern scientific studies, it has been clarified that many Buddhist sutras were written in later periods by various great priests in India and China. However, so long as they conform to the Truth which was found by Sakyamuni, it can be said that they are Buddhist teachings. In connection with such an understanding of Buddhism, it is naturally admitted that many sects and schools arose in later periods in Buddhism in accordance with the ability of the followers.

For example, in the Kamukra period of Japan, Pure Land Buddhism such as the Jodo and Shin sects were founded for the common people who could not practise any hard discipline or meditation in their daily lives, and also who could not understand any profound doctrines of Buddhism. On the other hand, Zen Buddhism, such as the Soto and Rinzai sects, were transmitted from China and prospered as the practice of meditation among the warrior class who earnestly desired some religious practices as the background of their everyday life. At the same time, old Buddhist sects, such as the Tendai and Shingon which were founded in the Heian period before Kamakura, still possessed strong power and influence among the aristocrats who greatly appreciated the traditional doctrines and rituals of Buddhism for the purpose of protecting the nation by Buddhism.

In the case of Kamakura Buddhism of Japan, each one of the sects and schools is the manifestation of the Truth first expounded by Sakyamuni Buddha, and, of course, each of them had its own *raison d'être*.

I have already mentioned above important doctrines and the standpoint of Buddhism. Now let us investigate the Buddhist interpretation of the meaning and purpose of life from the standpoint of these Buddhist doctrines and views.

MEANING AND PURPOSE OF LIFE

First of all again we should realize the fact that all existences and phenomena of this world are impermanent and non-substantial. Then what will be the meaning and purpose of life in such a temporal and changing world? What will be the correct way to live in this impermanent society?

According to Buddhist understanding, all worldly happiness —such as marriage, wealth, status and even having lovely children—is but temporal and the cause of pain and suffering. Then what will be the real happiness which will never be the cause of suffering in this present society?

Before I answer these questions, I would like to explain the Buddhist interpretation or way of thinking about everyday phenomena by showing a few examples.

Here is an apple. For those who like it this apple is precious and worthy of appreciation, while for those who dislike it, this apple will be neither delicious nor worthy of appreciation.

Again for those whose country produces a lot of apples, this apple will be not so precious, and for those whose country does not produce apples, this must be valuable and precious irrespective of the likes and dislikes of people.

When one who usually likes apples very much has eaten a lot of apples already and does not feel any hunger, then this apple will be not precious for him at that moment. On the contrary, when one who usually dislikes apples is in the state of starvation, this apple must be a precious and valuable food to sustain his life at this moment.

Similarly, the evaluation and appraisal of existence in this world is always changing in accordance with the condition, circumstances, situation, and so on.

For those who earnestly desire to have a baby, the birth of a baby will be the greatest pleasure and happiness in this world. But one will surely feel that it is discouraging to have a baby after he has had a dozen children.

Such happiness as is shown above is not real happiness as the evaluation of the same phenomenon or the same thing is always changing according to his condition and situation.

In order to make clear this Buddhist interpretation of worldly phenomena, another example is shown in the following.

Here is a person who is sitting in the seat of the tourist class of an airplane. He may think how happy he is because he had enough money to buy a tourist-class ticket. This man will probably think in his mind that there must be many people in the world who because of their poverty cannot even buy tickets on trains or buses. Or he may think how pitiful he is because he did not have enough money to buy a first-class ticket on the plane. In the former case, he is surely in a state of happiness, while in the latter case he is in the state of unhappiness. He who thinks how happy he is, is surely happier than the person who, even though he has first-class accommodation on a plane, is constantly fretting about how busy he is. However, if the person who is now in the tourist class feeling how happy he is, would become poor and could not even buy a tourist class ticket on a plane, then he would become unhappy. So, his happiness in the tourist class is the relative happiness which is temporal and impermanent. Therefore, he will surely be in the state of unhappiness when his condition or situation is changed. Buddhists are not pursuing such a relative happiness which is always changing in accordance with the difference of condition.

Then, what will be the attitude of Buddhists in these cases and what will be the state of real happiness for Buddhists?

According to Buddhist interpretation, real happiness always lies in the midst of the everyday life of every person only when he can observe existence and phenomena of this world as they are. If one could feel happiness in any case and condition, it can be said that he is in the state of real happiness. He will be satisfied with any situation and condition. When he is in the first-class of a plane, when he is in the tourist class of a plane, when he is in the train, when he is in the bus, when he is in his home, when he is in any place, he shall be able to be in the state of happiness, because such happiness is not relative happiness which can be felt only through comparing oneself with the other people. Is it possible to be in the state of such happiness in the worst condition for human beings? Such a question will naturally arise among the readers.

Now, I must quote again the passage of reliance on the three holy treasures of Buddhism which I quoted already at the beginning of this essay.

"How fortunate I was to be born a human being! It is the hardest of the hardest things to be born a human being. Again how fortunate I was to be given a chance to know Buddhism! It is also very seldom that one is given a chance to know it."

When one feels strong thankfulness for the fact that he could be born a human being and again for the fact that he was given the chance to know Buddhism, then it is natural that he is always in the state of real happiness even if he were in the midst of the worst condition of his life. Through the realization that it is the hardest of the hardest things in the world to be born a human being, all his worldly dissatisfactions and unhappiness will be extinguished. Such a happiness is not relative or worldly happiness but is real happiness.

If one could be in a state of real happiness in any circumstances, probably you may ask "then is it not necessary for man to endeavour to make his life better?"

Buddhism never denies the effort of men or it can even be said, according to Buddhism, that each human being has to try to do his best in the present society. Why?

Here we have to recollect the concepts of mutual relationship and dependent origination of all existences and phenomena of this world.

Buddhism, especially Mahayana Buddhism, is not an egoistic religion but an altruistic religion. Therefore, each individual has to try to lead all people, irrespective of religion, to the state of real happiness. We human beings cannot live in this society by ourselves as we are chained by innumerable direct and indirect causes and as there is not even a single person who has nothing to do with us. When we could realize this, we cannot be satisfied with our own happiness. Each one of us has to try to do our best to lead all other people to the state of real happiness and the final state of Buddhism, Nirvana.

If one could realize the fact that present deeds will not only direct him in the future, but also be an indirect influence on all others in the future, he cannot do anything without being most careful to do his best at all times.

Therefore, the attitude in everyday life of Buddhists is to do one's best in every deed, being in the state of real happiness.

Before concluding, I would like to mention the Buddhist understanding of other religions.

There are many ways to reach the summit of a mountain

For those who are weak, aged, and too young, it will be almost impossible to climb up the steep cliff even if it would be the shortcut to the summit. For those who are young and strong enough, it will be tiresome and dissatisfactory to walk along the plain and wide road to the summit. We can choose any way to climb up the mountain. But if we choose the wrong way, we should not be able to ever attain the top. In the case of a mountain, there will be several ways leading to the summit for each person. However, in the case of religion, there must be only one way for a person that leads to enlightenment or salvation in which one can find out the real happiness and the meaning and purpose of life.

As mentioned above, one of the important standpoints of Buddhism is to admit various teachings in accordance with the ability of men. The same consideration is possible in the case of other religions.

According to the Buddhist way of thinking, all religions which are aiming at right enlightenment and realization possess their own *raison d'être,* because each religion is necessary for those who could not be enlightened or saved by other religions.

Do not be disappointed, all you who have failed to have the faith in one religion! Try to continue to find out the religion which is suitable to your ability, comprehension, circumstances, nationality, education, state of mind, age and condition, and also in which you can find out the meaning and purpose of life as well as real happiness.

It will be the duty of religionists, such as priests and pastors, to make it possible for those who are trying to find out their own religion to search where they will.

The above-mentioned interpretation is the Buddhist understanding of the meaning of the existence of other religions.

According to Buddhism, the religion for each person to rely upon and follow will depend upon his ability as well as innumerable direct and indirect causes of his own and all others in the connection of mutual relationship.

In my case, for example, I was born of my father, a Buddhist priest and a Buddhist scholar, and therefore, I was brought up in Buddhist surroundings. After I grew up, I studied various Buddhist doctrines of different sects and schools as well as the doctrines of other religions. Finally, I myself found out and realized that I was only one of the common men who could not do any hard practices or meditation and also could not realize any difficult doctrine of Buddhism in everyday life, although I could understand them in my mind. I could understand various doctrines of Buddhist sects and schools as well as doctrines of other religions only as philosophy and ideas, but I could not realize them as my own religion. Through these direct and indirect causes as well as my own ability, I came to possess a strong conviction that it is only the path of the Shin sect of Pure Land Buddhism which could lead me to perfect salvation. Therefore, I am a follower of the Shin sect.

However, this is only my case. For other persons, there must be different ways to follow as their ability and causes will be different from those of my own. Needless to say, the way which one man follows is not necessarily the way for others. Food which is delicious for one is not always delicious for others.

One may choose Christianity for his religion to follow through his ability and innumerable causes as well as his background in society. Another may choose Shinto for his religion. The most important thing for an individual is to find out the religion which is most suitable for him.

Religions should not be too illiberal or narrow-minded in their general standpoint. Nevertheless the faith of each individual should be absolute and uncompromising.

In conclusion, I will clarify the Buddhist interpretation of the problem of Meaning and Purpose in Life.

According to the Buddhist standpoint, the meaning of life is to realize that it is only possible for one to live in this present world through innumerable direct and indirect causes which came from all others. And the purpose of life is to live every-day, or even every moment, in the consciousness of how I am happy to be born a human being and that every deed will be the indirect cause for others in the future. That is to say, to live in the state of real happiness through the realization of the impermanence and non-substantiality of existences and phenomena of this world, and to live in the hearty gratitude to all other existences is the purpose of life: and to live in this present society as a human being itself is the meaning of life.

Of course, to find real happiness in this actual life, which is full of worldly desires, is very difficult, or it can even be said that it is almost impossible, because we human beings are apt to become attached to the sources of worldly happiness such as money, property, position and so on, even if we could fully understand that they are temporal and non-substantial.

For those who really realize the truth that life is impermanent and existences and phenomena of this world are non-substantial, even death, which is generally considered as the greatest sorrow in human life, must be accepted as one phenomenon of this impermanent world. Nevertheless, I am sure that most people feel the greatest fear when they realize that they are going to die or going to be killed soon.

However, there is no other way to live in this present world than to follow the way of life in which one tries to find real happiness in the midst of sorrow, suffering, pain, agony, and worldly pleasures and happiness.

We Buddhists will try to continue to find out the real happiness in this present world realizing that we were fortunately born human beings and fortunately given the chance to know Buddhism until the last moment of our lives.

We appreciate every existence and phenomenon of this world as they are chained to our existence and everyday life.

This is the Buddhist interpretation of the problem of the Meaning and Purpose of Life." That is to say, there is no other meaning and purpose of life than to live as a human being seeing all existences and phenomena as they are.

IV. JUDAISM

Faith, like metaphysics, is concerned with the meaning of life.
Because both are involved with the Ultimate, neither can rest
with the finite purposes achieved by human action, or with such
limited significance as is disclosed by random experience. What
is at stake in both is *one* meaning, not many haphazard and fragmented meanings, and of *all* of life, not of its high points only.

But the religious differs from the metaphysical quest. Metaphysics attempts to rise above life in order to grasp its meaning
in speculative thought. Faith remains in the midst of life and
comes upon meaning within it. The metaphysician questions;
the believer finds himself questioned. And whereas the one
answers his questions with theories and explanations, the other
answers, to being questioned, with his very life. *The core of the
religious reality is a meeting between the Divine and the human,
and religious meaning is found in and through this meeting and
nowhere else.* Thus the Biblical creation-myth is no "explanation of cosmic origins," nor does the Book of Job "solve the
problem of evil." The one reflects an encounter with a Creator
forcing man to accept radical creatureliness—both the world's
and his own; the other reflects an encounter with a just Power
—in the midst of an evil which, however real, destroys neither
the justice nor the power.

Religions—which differ in much else—differ in substance
according to their experience and understanding of the Divine-
human meeting: whether, when and how it occurs, and what
happens in it. In Judaism,[1] the fundamental and all-penetrating
occurrence is a primordial mystery, and a miracle of miracles.

---

[1] This essay relies, in addition to the Hebrew Bible, mainly on the
Rabbinic sources, which in Judaism are second in importance only to
the Bible itself. These are here given special emphasis because, unlike
the Bible, they are not well known. Since these sources are not easily
accessible, all references are confined to Montefiore-Loewe, *A Rabbinic
Anthology* (London: Macmillan and Co., 1938) (henceforth referred
to as *RA*), a truly outstanding collection.

he Divine, though dwelling on high and infinitely above the human, yet bends down low so as to accept and confirm the human in his finite humanity; and the human, though met by Divine Infinity, yet may and must respond to this meeting out of the midst of his finiteness.

Some scholars attribute to the God of early Jewish faith mythological finitude. But this reflects blindness to the religious realities of Judaism, due to modern prejudice. Even in pristine beginnings the Jewish God is the all-demanding God; and it is only a question of time until the only-important God becomes the only-existing God. Hence even his earliest followers smash the idols: Judaism is anti-mythological from the start.[2]

Just as the God even of "primitive" Judaism is infinite, so the man even of "advanced" Judaism remains finite. Man, though the Divine image, remains a creature; he is neither a fragment of Divinity nor potentially Divine. Such notions— the product of modern humanism—remain unassimilable to the Jewish faith; and where they are allowed to enter into its heart they are destructive of it.[3] The Divine-human meeting remains a reality whereever Judaism is a living religion; and the miracle of miracles which has been referred to remains its core.

For this reason, Jewish life and thought are marked by a fundamental tension. This might have been evaded in one of two ways. It might have been held that the Divine and the human are, after all, incapable of meeting, as are the views, for example, of ancient Epicureanism and modern Deism. But this is consistently rejected in Jewish tradition, which considers Epicureanism tantamount to atheism. Or it might have been held that the meeting is a mystic conflux, in which the finite

---

[2]Martin Buber's *The Prophetic Faith* (New York: Macmillan, 1949) shows that the critical view which ascribes to the Biblical faith an evolution" from "polytheism" via "henotheism" toward a "pure monotheism" sheds far less light on the Bible than on the unconscious assumptions of the respective critics. Y. Kaufmann's *The Religion of Israel* (University of Chicago Press: Chicago, 1960) argues that Biblical religion is so far from being simply "influenced" by the pagan religions of its time as to fail even to understand them.

[3]Expressions such as "the Divine in man" are found in the reform Jewish *Union Prayer Boom* (CCAR: Cincinnati 1946, p. 7); but they remain extraneous to its spirit.

dissolves into the Infinite and man suffers loss of his very humanity. But this, although a profound religious possibility and a serious challenge, is rejected in Judaism as well. Such thinkers as Maimonides,[4] Isaac Luria[5] and the Baal Shem Tob[6] all stop short—albeit on occasion but barely—of embracing mysticism. And those who do not—such as Spinoza—pass beyond the bounds of Judaism. The Infinity of the Divine, the finiteness of the human and the meeting between them: these all remain, then, wherever Judaism preserves its substance; and the mystery and tension of this meeting permeates all else.

Hence whatever meaning life acquires derives from this meeting. Primordial meaning, however, lies in the meeting itself. This meaning is of *human* life; for the Divine accepts and confirms the human in the moment of meeting. It cannot however, lie in some finite human purpose, supposedly more ultimate than the meeting and merely established by it. For what could be more ultimate than the Presence of God? Thus before the goodness of creation lies in anything else, it lies in that the Divine has created it, and this is a truth originally bound up with the moment of its disclosure. Thus, too, the Psalmist finds meaning in the Divine omnipresence in both Heaven and the netherworld, not in something else of which it merely gives assurance (Ps. 139). And when he comes upon God even in the valley of the shadow of death (Ps. 23), he does not learn either that there is no death, or that it is no evil, but rather that it need not be feared, and indeed can no longer be feared. The Presence of God, then, is an *"inexpressible* confirmation of meaning . . . The question of the meaning of life is no longer there. But were it there, it would not have to be answered."[7]

৵৹

[4] The greatest medieval Jewish philosopher, 1135-1204.

[5] The redactor of the Kabbalah, 1534-1572.

[6] "The Lord of the Good Name," Israel Ben Eliezer, founder of Hasidism, 1699-1760.

[7] Martin Buber, *I and Thou* (New York: Charles Scribner's Sons 1958) p. 110. The italics are ours.

But in Judaism the inexpressible confirmation of meaning also assumes expression; and this is because the Divine-human meeting assumes structure and content.

First, it is a universal human experience that times of Divine presence do not last forever. This experience, however, does not everywhere have the same significance or even reality. Conceivably mythological religions—for which the world is "full of gods" (Thales)—may find Divinity even in the most worldly preoccupation with the most finite ends: this is not possible if the Divine is an Infinity other than all things finite. Mystical religions, on their part, might dispatch into mere appearance all such preoccupations, and confine reality to the moment in which the human dissolves into the Divine: this is not possible if the moment of Divine-human meeting itself confirms the human in his human finitude. The human has reality at all times of his finite existence; and yet these include times in which he is divorced from the Divine. The God of Judaism then, while "near" at times, is "far" at other times, whatever the causes of such farness. Times of Divine farness too must have meaning; for the far God remains an existing God, and nearness remains an ever-live possibility. But they derive their meaning from times of Divine nearness. The dialect between Divine nearness and Divine farness is all-pervasive in Jewish experience; and it already points to an eschatological future in which it is overcome.[8]

---

[8] The expressions "Divine nearness" and "Divine farness", common in Rabbinic literature, have two Jewish connotations. The first, which is primary, is expressed in the following passage: "The idol is near, and yet is far. God is far (for is He not in the heaven of heavens?), and yet He is near . . . For a man enters a synagogue, and stands behind a pillar, and prays in a whisper, and God hears his prayer . . . Can there be a nearer God than this? He is as near to His creatures as the ear to the mouth" (RA., p. 22). The Divine is at once radically other than man and the world, and yet immediately present.

It is in their second connotation, however, that the expressions "Divine nearness" and "Divine farness" are used in these pages. The Biblical and Rabbinic God may "hide His Face", e.g., be not immediately religiously available (e.g., Ps. 13: 2; 44: 35; 69: 18). Divine farness of this kind is at times due to human sin, but at others simply inexplicable.

Still a third possible sense of Divine farness—a Heideggerian "absence" which has at least temporarily abandoned the world—has no Jewish warrant; and the term "absent God" is used in these pages only to be rejected.

Secondly, the Divine-human meeting assumes structure and content through the way in which the human is accepted and confirmed in his humanity. In Judaism the Divine accepts and confirms the human by *commanding* him in his humanity; it thus makes him responsible in the very presence of Divinity, and the response called for is *obedience* to Divinity out of the midst of man's humanity. Here lies the ground for the Jewish rejection, already referred to, of the mystic surrender. The human *must* remain human because in commanding him *as* human this Presence accepts him in his humanity. In Judaism Divine Grace is not superadded and subservient to Divine Commandment only. It already is, primordially, *in* the commandment, and were it not so the commnadment would be radically incapable of human performance. It is in the Divine Law itself that the Psalmist finds his delight, not only in a Divine action subsequent to its observance (Ps. 119.91); and if it saves him from perishing in his affliction it is because Divine Love has handed it over to humans—not to angels—[9] thereby making it in principle capable of human fulfilment.[10]

Because the Divine acceptance of the human is a commanding acceptance, the inexpressible meaning of the Divine-human meeting assumes four interrelated expressions of which two are immediately in the commandment itself. First, Divine commandment is itself a dimension of meaning; for to be a human commanded by the Divine is to be accepted as humanly responsible. It is only a question of time for the one commanding Presence to give utterance to many specific commandments, which specify Divine acceptance and human responsibility according to the exigencies of space and time.

Secondly, meaning is transferred to the side of the human.

---

[9]According to Rabbinic legend the angels offer to perform the commandments in Israel's stead but are told that inasmuch as they do not eat and procreate they cannot perform those commandments connected with food and procreation.

[10]For a fuller development of this point, cf. my article "Kant and Judaism" (*Commentary*, vol. 36, 1963, pp. 460-467).

For if to be Divinely commanded is to be both obligated and able to obey, then meaning is capable of human realization, and his meaning is real even in the sight of Divinity. The fear induced in the finite human by the Infinite Divine Presence may seem to destroy any such presumption. Yet the acceptance of the human by the commanding Love makes possible, and indeed mandatory, human self-acceptance. Even for the sceptical author of the Book of Ecclesiastes it is the conjunction of the fear of God and the obedience to his commandments which is the "whole man."[11]

A third aspect of meaning comes into view because the Divine commandment initiates a *mutual* Divine-human relationship. The God of Judaism is no Deistic First Cause, which, having caused the world, goes into perpetual retirement. Neither is he a Law-Giver who, having given Laws, leaves man's response in human solitariness. Along with commandment, handed over for human action, goes the promise of a *Divine* action, and this makes itself contingent on the human action so as to establish a mutual relationship. God gives to man a *covenant*, i.e. a contract, and he does not contract out of its terms, but becomes a partner.

The Divine-human meeting, however, has yet a fourth expression; and unless this had gradually emerged, the Jewish faith could hardly have survived through the centuries. A mutual relation between an Infinite Divinity and a finite humanity has become possible despite its paradox; for a pristine Divine love has accepted the human. Even so, that relation remains destructible at finite hands and, were it *simply* mutual, it would be destroyed by man almost the moment it were established. Even in earlier forms of Jewish faith, God remains long-suffering enough to put up with persistent human failures; and at length it becomes clear that the covenant can survive only

[11]Eccl. 12: 13. The question whether this passage is a later addition to the original text is irrelevant in the present context.

if God's patience is absolute. The covenant, to be sure, *remains* mutual; and Divine action remains part of this mutuality, as reaction to human action. But Divine action also breaks through this limitation and maintains the covenant in *unilateral* love. The human race after Noah, and Israel at least since the time of Jeremiah, still can—and do—rebel against their respective covenants with God. But they can no longer destroy them (Gen. 8.15 ff., Jer. 31). Sin still causes God to punish Israel; but no conceivable sin on Israel's part can cause him to forsake her. Unilateral Divine love has made the covenant indestructible.

In Judaism, covenantal existence becomes a continuous, uninterrupted way of life. This is possible because the four described expressions of meaning become integrated with the dialectic between Divine nearness and Divine farness, already expounded. A Divine-human relation unstructured by commandment would alternate between times of inexpressible meaning and times of sheer waiting for such meaning. A relationship so structured, but failing to encompass both Divine nearness and farness, could not extend its scope over the whole of human life. If confined to times of Divine nearness, covenantal existence would be shattered into as many fragments as there are moments of Divine nearness, with empty spaces between them. If confined to Divine farness it would degenerate, on the Divine side, into an external law santioned by an absent God and, on the human side, into legalistic exercises practised in His absence.[12] But as understood and lived in Judaism, covenantal existence persists in times of Divine farness. The commandment is still present, as is the Divine promise, however obscured in its content. The human power to perform the commandment while impaired, is not destroyed; and he who cannot perform the commandment for the sake of God is nevertheless bidden to perform it. Such performance, which is not for his sake, will lead to performance which *is* for his sake.[13] Times of Divine

---

[12]*Supra,* note 8.

[13]On this subject, cf. the whole of chapter X in *RA.*

nearness, then, do not light up themselves alone. Their meaning extends over all of life.

❧

So much for the general characteristics of the Divine-human relationship according to Judaism. What humans are partners of such relationships? Individuals or communities? And some individuals and communities only or, potentially, the whole human race? It will become evident that in Judaism these are not mutually exclusive alternatives, and indeed, that those modern conceptions which would make them so—"individualism" vs. "collectivism," and "particularism" vs. "universalism" —are alien to the dynamic of the Jewish faith.

Consider, first, "universalism" and "particularism." *Because the God of the Divine-human meeting is Infinite, each meeting discloses him—potentially at least—as the One of every meeting. Because the man of this meeting is finite, and accepted in his finitude, each meeting singles him out—potentially at least— as a unique individual or a unique group.* Mythological deities may remain "particularistic," i.e., confined to specific limits of time and space; the Jewish God who smashes the idols breaks through such limits. The mystical conflux may dissolve the here-and-now into a "universalistic" eternity; the Jewish encounter with God accentuates the here-and-now in which it occurs. For in this singled-out man is bidden to obey the Divine commandment. Unless from the start transcending the here-and-now of meeting the Jewish God would fragment himself into "moment-gods"[14] according to the moments of meeting; and unless throughout every meeting capable of singling out—*this* individual, *this* people, here and now—he would accept not existing humans but only unreal abstractions. The Biblical God is indeed the God of all the nations; but there

---

[14]The expression is Martin Buber's, *Between Man and Man* (Beacon Press: Boston, 1955), p. 15.

is no word for the abstraction "mankind" in the Hebrew Scriptures.

To be singled out by the Divine is a crucial and persisting Jewish experience. The first commandment given to the first Jew—that Abraham leave his country (Gen. 12:1-4)—is addressed to him only; it does not call for a universal peoples' migration. The commandment to become a holy people unto God (Exod. 16:6) constitutes Israel as a unique people; it is not an application of a universal principle. The rabbis teach that God has made each man unique and speaks to him in his uniqueness (*RA*, pp. 33, 103); and this teaching is powerfully reaffirmed in modern Hasidism. To be singled out is, so to speak, built into Jewish existence even today. Some modern Jewish thinkers have identified the "essence" of Judaism with universal moral and religious principles shared by all higher religions; but although taking great pains to connect this "universal" essence with the "particular" existence of the Jewish people, their efforts end in failure.[15]

Just as the human remains singled out even in the most "advanced" Jewish experience, so God transcends, even in the most "primitive" Jewish experience, the here-and-now in which His singling-out acts occur. The significance of the commandment addressed to Abraham is fulfilled only in future generations. The covenant between God and Israel has from the outset a scope which transcends Israel; and it is only a question of time until this scope encompasses the whole human race. And the Talmud teaches that one man who in one single action saves one single human life is regarded as though he had saved all human lives (*RA*, p. 103).

"Universalism" and "particularism," then, are not only both

---

[15]This is especially true of the reconstructionist philosophy of Mordecai Kaplan which, having defined religious truth in purely universal terms, goes on to insist that this abstract truth has, and must have, particular embodiment in diverse "religious civilizations." It is unable to say what obligates Jews to remain true to their "Jewish civilization," when what it embodies are truths which all higher religions have in common.

present throughout Jewish religious experience; they are also internally united. Their union is manifest in *history*. History is not history unless each of its events is unique; and it remains fragmented into many histories unless these unique events are, nevertheless, one "universal" whole. In Judaism, the events of history become one whole because history assumes *direction* given it by Divine incursions into it. The Jewish God is from the start a God of history; and it is only a question of time until he becomes the Lord of *all* history, encompassing not only the whole past but the whole future as well, including its Messianic consummation.

A crucial dimension of meaning in Judaism is therefore historical. This meaning structures itself according to the realities previously described. First, the Divine commandment becomes historical. The Hebrew prophets do not proclaim a universally applicable Divine will only. It is their inescapable agony to be men of their time. Jeremiah demands passive submission to the enemy, well aware that armed resistance has been the Divine will at other times. And as he is confronted by another would-be prophet with the opposite counsel, it is his unavoidable suffering—and that of the people addressed—that no resort to general principles will settle the issue between them (Jer. 27, 28). This issue may indeed be settled by the future. But by then it will be too late for an action which is needed now; so radically singled-out and singling-out can be a prophetic message. And yet, though a man of his time, the prophet is not for his time alone. His moment is an epoch-making moment significant for all of history.

Secondly, the commandment establishes the historical meaning of human action, without which, indeed, the meaning of history would hardly be historical. A Providence which in pursuit of its historical purpose reduced man to a will-less automaton would not be a Providence which governed history but rather a blind Fate which destroyed it. The prophets do not predict an inescapable future. Their predictions—such as they are—are contingent upon human action. Human action, then, assumes a decisive historical meaning; and it is no less epoch-making than the prophetic message which demands it. And when it becomes world-historical it leaves indelible marks on all future history.

But this would be impossible if history were composed of human action only, albeit responding to a commendment which is Divine. Human action is finite: how can it assure a direction of history, or leave indelible marks upon it? Only if it is not left to itself but in persistent mutuality with a Divine action which reacts to it. In Judaism, the Divine-human mutuality, above described, becomes a historical reality. Such early Jewish documents as the Book of Judges can see an exact historical correlation between Israel's obedience and God-given victories, and between Israel's defiance and God-sent defeats. And, naive though this may seem, *some* significant correlation—precarious, fragmentary and ambiguous—remains in all subsequent forms of the Jewish faith. A history dependent for meaning on human action alone would lead to despair. And a Divine action in history devoid of all reference to human action would deprive this latter of meaning.

But the naive view of history reflected in the Book of Judges does not remain the Jewish view. Subsequent faith modifies it in three main respects. First, we have already noted how in Judaism Divine action, mutually related to the human and contingent upon it, is gradually seen to have an aspect of uni-lateralness as well. Such Divine unilateral action comes to be part of the Jewish understanding of history, and traces of it are already present in the Book of Judges itself: behind the Divine punishment which is a reaction to man's sinful action is a Divine unilateral action—a Love which seeks to produce repentance. Such a Love, to be sure, is not understood as wholly unilateral so long as it is considered possible that sufficiently grave sins on Israel's part might cause God to abandon or destroy his covenant with her. But at least from Jeremiah on Jewish faith rules this possibility out.

In Rabbinic literature, the togetherness of Divine-human mutuality and Divine unilateralness becomes the object of explicit theological reflection. God is Judge, and God is Father; and unless he were both the world could not exist. God is Judge: a Love without Judgment would destroy the distinction between the righteous and the wicked, and hence all responsible action. God is Father: a Judgment without Love would place on human responsibility a greater burden than it can bear. But the relationship between Divine Judgment and Divine Love is past finite understanding.[16]

Secondly, the relation between Divine omnipotence and human freedom is not problematic in early Biblical experience. The Book of Judges harmonizes with ease a Divine power encompassing all history with a human freedom to rebel against it. For its interest is confined to Israel; and it sees Divine power as reacting to Israel's acting. It is hardly necessary to add that abstract reflections on human freedom and Divine power are beyond its ken.

But later Biblical writings reflect the awareness that a Providence limited by human acting would lose its providential character. They might, therefore, have been confronted with a dilemma—either human freedom vanishes, and Providence becomes blind fate, or else freedom remains, and Divine power is reduced to finitude, thus governing history no more. Biblical thought does not reflect on this dilemma; for it is not philosophical thought. It does, however, immediately reject both of its horns. Nebukadnezzar is the instrument of a Divine Providence which uses him to punish Israel. Yet he remains a free and responsible agent, hence is punished for his sins (Jer. 25:9,ff.)

---

[16]E.g., *RA.*, pp. 73 ff. I have treated this subject more fully in my article "Self-realization and the Search for God" (*Judaism* Vol. I, 1952, pp. 299 ff).

That such a relation is paradoxical is explicitly recognized in Rabbinic reflection. But this latter—which is no more philosophical than Biblical immediacy—agrees with the Bible in rejecting the dilemma. Human action limits Divine Power, which is why men "strengthen" it when they obey the Divine will and 'weaken" it when they disobey it. It limits Divine Power, however, "as it were" only: finite man cannot literally either weaken or strengthen the Infinite God. And yet human thought must remain with such symbolic statements which reflect paradox. It cannot rise to a literal truth which is free of it (*RA.*, pp. 33 ff.). For man must remain with this double truth that "everything is foreseen, yet freedom of choice is given" (*RA.*, p. 36).

This implies that history is wholly in Divine hands even while man has a share in its making; that, whereas righteousness makes man a partner in the realization of the Divine plan, sin, for all its reality and power, is unable to disrupt or destroy it.

There is still a third respect in which the fully developed Jewish understanding of history departs from the Book of Judges: the naive view of the latter is refuted by historical experience. Jeremiah complains that the way of the wicked prospers (Jer. 12, 1). And the whole Book of Job is the classical Jewish refutation of the belief—persisting elsewhere, and in secular form, even in modern times—that all prosperity and good fortune is a merited reward, hence in itself proof of virtue; and that all adversity and disaster is a deserved punishment, hence in itself proof of vice. The experience giving rise to such complaints might have been belittled either by the admonition to worry about virtue only, and not its reward, or by the restriction of meaning in history to a spiritual dimension, exclusive of all worldly fortune both good and ill. But while Jewish thought does give the first admonition[17] it rejects

---

[17] Cf. *Pirke Abot* I 3 (*RA.*, p. 213): "Be not like servants who serve their Master for the sake of a reward, but like servants who serve with no thought of reward."

any suggestion that history is not, after all, in Divine hands; and as for the restriction of significant history to a spiritual aspect, Judaism throughout its history wholly repudiates it. The complaint of Jeremiah and Job, then, cannot be evaded; and with this the Jewish quest for meaning in history comes upon limitations.

Two such limitations are, in fact, already implied in the foregoing exposition. If Divine omnipotence co-exists with human freedom; if Divine power is manifest in what yet remains the criminal act of a Nebukadnezzar—or, for that matter, the righteous act of an Abraham or a Moses—: then meaning in history, even if and when disclosed, is disclosed only within the bounds of finite understanding; and this falls radically short of the understanding of God.

Secondly, meaning in history is not everywhere disclosed. Nebukadnezzar is seen as serving a Divine purpose; but not every tyrant is a Nebukadnezzar. And while a prophet proclaims its task to one generation most generations are lacking in prophets. In such times, however, men are not left with their own wisdom only, when engaged in historical action; nor are they forced to deny meaning to history where none is disclosed. For the God far at such times remains an existing God, and one able to turn near again. This doctrine, previously expounded, has a twofold application to meaning in history. First, even though God is far, his commandment is still near; it is not on his own counsel alone that man falls back in fathoming the task of the present hour. Secondly, the events of the present, although *disclosing* no meaning, yet do *possess* meaning. For history remains in God's hands even when all is dark.

This distinction between meaning and disclosed meaning in history is crucial in Judaism, and few distinctions have been more vital in the history of its survival. Its loss would have left Jews with three alternatives. They might have identified meaning in history with what history discloses, and celebrated naked success: but how could they have done so and yet resisted Babylonians and Romans in the name of their faith? Or they might have abandoned history as a sphere of religious meaning: but how could they have done so and yet carried forward a religious existence inextricably bound up with history? Finally, they might have distinguished between a sacred history in the keeping of God and a secular history outside the Divine concern. But such a distinction no Jew ever accepted as absolute. For no Jewish thinker ever regarded the "secular"—whether in or outside of history—as beyond the Divine care. Nor could he have done so and remained true to fundamental Jewish realities. The pristine Divine-human meeting in Judaism accepts the human in his psychosomatic totality; and the Divine commandment specified itself socially, politically and economically, as well as individually and spiritually. A meaning at once manifest in history and yet indifferent to poverty, war and tyranny is Jewishly unthinkable.

One cannot, then, exaggerate the importance in Judaism of the distinction between meaning and disclosed meaning in history. Without it, the Jewish people could hardly have survived, at once sure of the persistence of their covenant with God throughout every calamity, and yet existing *in* the history in which such calamities occurred,—not shut off from it by monastic walls.

But there is yet a third limitation to the Jewish search for meaning in history, and this only gradually emerges. Not only is the *disclosure* of meaning in history fragmentary; the meaning *itself* is fragmentary; and past and present point not only to a finite future but to one which is absolute and all-consummating as well. Not until an eschatological dimension comes into view is the Jewish understanding of meaning in history complete.

The reasons for the emergence of this dimension can be more fully understood only later on. One reason, however, is already implied in the foregoing. A Jeremiah sure of history, and ignorant only of some of its content, would not contend with God but merely seek Divine enlightenment. And a Job filled with the same conviction would begin where in fact he ends: with the incommensurability of the Divine dispensation with all things human. Both Jeremiah and Job, however, are forced to do their contending. This latter, never forgotten in subsequent Judaism, is, in fact, rooted in the pristine Jewish experience. Divine Love has singled out man so as to make him humanly responsible; it is not bound, then, to the consequences of its own action,—to a Divine Justice not *wholly* incommensurate with responsible human action? Jews were forced to go beyond acceptance of an undisclosed meaning in history. They were bound to question meaning in history itself, in the light of the historical realities. This questioning, to be sure, did not result in a wholesale scepticism, and a despair of meaning in history. But it did result in the belief that meaning has remained incomplete in past history, and will remain so in a future no different from the past.

The question to be asked of Judaism, then, is not so much why the Messianic belief appeared on the scene. It is, much rather, why it appeared so late. Is the prosperity of the wicked or the suffering of the righteous so rare a phenomenon, or one so difficult to perceive? Can even the naive author of the Book of Judges have been unacquainted with it, or unable to recognize its implications?

A partial answer—albeit partial only—is probably that for early Biblical man the meaning of a life which remains incomplete can find completion in the lives of others. If Abraham dies satisfied it is because of a Divine promise extending to his descendants (Gen. 12: 2; 25: 7). If the Book of Judges perceives complete justice in history it is at least partly because justice is due to the people only, not to the individuals who compose it. Early Biblical man takes no offence at a God who punishes the children for the sins of the fathers (Exod. 20: 5):

and here lies one reason why a finite future can consummate the meaning of past and present.

But the God of Jeremiah and especially Ezekiel will not tolerate the death of the children for their fathers' sins (Jer. 31: 29-30; Ez. 18): the God of Israel is God of each person as well. Once this has become the explicit Jewish faith—it has long been implicit in it—the contention of Jeremiah and Job has become inescapable. Men *do* suffer unjustly in their individual lives; and this suffering cannot acquire meaning through historical events beyond their death. Meaning in history, then, is fragmentary, and is left so by a future no different from the past. Thus an eschatological future comes into view. Even such a future, however, if historical, will not silence the complaint on behalf of the individual. We must shortly consider the Messianic hope. But we see even now that Judaism, though an historical religion, is bound to reject a panhistoricism which would make individuals mere instruments in the achievement of history's Messianic end.

In the preceding section we have rejected the disjunction of "universalism" and "particularism," as alien to the dynamic and structure of the Jewish faith. We must now do the same with the disjunction of "collectivism" and "individualism." If Jewish faith ends up repudiating any reduction of the individual to his communal or historical role, then this repudiation is implicit in it from the beginning. For the pristine Divine-human meeting which accepts the human would not accept him wholly unless it encompassed, beside the community, the individual in his own right. There is Jewish authenticity to the rabbinic legend which makes the Sinaitic revelation address each individual Israelite (*RA.*, p. 33), as well as to the teaching that the Torah is given whenever men receive it (*RA.*, pp. 136 ff).

Aspects of such "individualism" are present even where the emphasis is "collectivistic." In binding the community the Mosaic code nevertheless recognizes the individual within it, which is why its scope extends beyond the community, to strangers and slaves. This motif becomes still more radical in post-Biblical thought. In the view of the Rabbis, the Divine spirit rests, according to their actions, on all individuals, whether they be Gentiles or Israelites, men or women, slaves or handmaids (*RA.*, p. 557); and the righteous among the Gentiles are priests of God (*RA.*, p. 671).

In consequence of such "individualism," historical change can hold no total sway over the commandments. Orthodox belief considers the Mosaic law to be, anyhow, exempt from historical change. All Jewish belief takes this view concerning those of its laws which state what is morally due to individuals: the wrongness of theft or murder does not depend on historical circumstances. The distinction between the historical and trans-historical commandments becomes fully explicit—and inescapable even for orthodox belief—in the case of the prophets. As we have said, these are men of their time; and Jeremiah proclaims submission to the enemy as the task of the hour when armed resistance has been the task of another hour. But it is unimaginable that he should take the same view regarding what is due to widows and orphans.

"Individualism" is as much present in Divine promise and its fulfilment as it is in the commandment. It is the individual who in the Psalms comes upon Divine salvation—both that which rewards human faithfulness (e.g. Ps. 15) and that which is the sheer gift of a gratuitous Love (e.g. Ps. 30, 130). Nor does this reflect an "individualistic" piety unrelated to, or even at odds with, the "collectivistic." It was in and for public worship that not a few Psalms were written; and they have retained an essential place in public Jewish worship until today. Indeed, the Jewish liturgy is so structured as to unite its communal and individual aspects in one whole. The God addressed as God of Abraham, Isaac and Jacob by the whole community is also addressed as *his* God by each individual member. And the Jewish calendar which includes Passover, celebrating the origin of the community of Israel, also includes the Day of Atonement, on which the individual stands before God in radical solitariness,—in the midst of the congregation. Within history the individual stands before a Judging and Gracious Presence which is Eternity.

But just as history comes at length to point to an eschatological dimension so does individual life. Early Biblical man may immediately rejoice in a commandment wholly fulfilled or in a salvation suddenly made manifest. In due course Jewish faith comes to accept that the saving moment does not vanquish evil permanently, nor absolutely even while the moment lasts; and that no mans is free of sin. To be sure, there is forgiveness wherever there is repentance, and a man ought to repent a day before his death. Yet repentance itself remains fragmentary, and even the most righteous of men—such as Abraham and Moses—do not die sinless (*RA.*, pp. 90, 306). The Pharisaic insistence on life after death is in the Jewish spirit; and there is poetic if not literal truth in the Rabbinic view that this belief is present in the Bible itself (*RA.*, pp. 599, 607).

❧

Since prophetic times Jewish faith looks to a Messianic future. This fulfills no longer limited goals only: a united people, a promised land, a central Sanctuary. The goals are all-encompassing. All nations flow to Jerusalem. The Kingdom of God is forever established; and it extends over the whole earth (e.g. Isa. 2: 2-4; 49: 1-6, Jer. 16: 19, Zach. 14: 9).

This is a hope for history. And it arises from a decisive historical experience: the promised land has been given and the central Sanctuary established; but the covenant has at best only a precarious life. Time and again Israel has returned to God only once more to forsake Him. And in the end the wearisome cycle is broken by catastrophe and exile.

It is doubtless original Jewish belief that the Divine commandment, once having accepted the human in his humanity is capable of total human performance; and that the Jewish commitment to the covenant, once made (especially Josh. 24), might have been kept with total fidelity. Under the impact of historical experience, however, the prophets are led to qualify this belief, and also to give Judaism a new dimension needed in the light of this qualification.

Israel has broken the covenant; she will always *sometimes* do so so long as she can. The Divine commandment leaves man able to sin; he will always sin so long as he is able: for sin, though not original, is nevertheless universal. The covenant, then, remains threatened, and from without as well as within. For the nations not only tempt Israel to idolatry but also endanger her very survival. History, in short, seems to have lost the direction it once had; and it will not re-acquire it from a future which is not qualitatively different from present and past.

In this situation, the prophets nevertheless reaffirm the ancient faith in the direction of history. *Revelation has initiated meaning in history: it points to a Redemption which will complete it.* The revealed commandment demands human performance; a Messianic Redemption will place the commandment into man's inward parts (Jer. 31: 33). Man has been able to obey the Divine will ever since the Divine commandment has accepted him in his humanity; in the Messianic future he will be neither willing nor able to disobey it. For all Nature will have been cured of its anti-divine potential: and the wolf will lie down with the lamb (Isa. 11: 6). And since Redemption will extend to all nations, it is all history which will find total consummation: the Kingdom of God on earth will be complete.

For such a future men are bound to wait, radically uncertain of the time of its arrival. For it is incommensurable with all human historical action. Throughout Jewish history, there seemed to be moments of human righteousness ripe for Redemption in the sight of Divine Justice, and long periods of human suffering ripe for it in the sight of Divine Compassion. But even popular legend came to picture the Messiah as bound in fetters,—anxious to come and yet held back by a God who alone knows the secret of the right time. And the Rabbis prohibited all attempts to calculate the end.

And yet men must work for the Messianic end even as they wait for it. A Messianic future simply incommmensurable with all historical human action would retroactively destroy the historical meaning which it were meant to consummate; yet if Jewish faith has come to expect this future at all it is precisely because meaning, however fragmentary, is nevertheless actual in pre-Messianic history. Hence men must, here and now, "prepare the world for the Kingdom of God;"[18] and it is on this goal that Jewish obedience to the commandments is in due course directed. And so aware does Jewish faith become of the weight of its Messianic obligation as to imagine that a single day of wholehearted obedience would cause the Messiah's immediate arrival (*RA.*, pp. 318, 583).

And yet the incommensurability of human action with its Messianic goal remains. Where, for one thing, is the individual or community capable of but a day's total faithfulness? How, for another, would the righteousness of some cause to cease all sinners,—to mention but one example, tyrannical rulers? The Messianic future, then, is at once connected with human action in pre-Messianic history and yet incommensurable with it.[19] The Messiah will arrive when the world has become good enough to make his coming possible; or evil enough to make

---

[18]An expression found in *Aleynu,* a prayer in the daily, Sabbath and Festival Liturgy.

[19]A statement by Rabbi Eleazar lists, as causes of redemption, side by side, events and actions in pre-Messianic history—"distress, prayer, the merit of the fathers, repentance"and "the end," functioning as an independent cause (*RA.*, p. 249).

it necessary. Men must act as though all depended on them; and wait and pray as though all depended on God.

Because the Messianic end is connected with present history the prophetic expectation can even now imagine it; because it remains incommensurable with all pre-Messianic history the prophetic imagination cannot make it literally intelligible. Thus the Messianic peace is no unearthly mystery but one in which men beat their swords into plowshares (Micah 4: 3; Isa. 2: 4). And the hunger stilled is not of the soul only but of the body as well (e.g Amos 9: 13-15). And yet such a peace and prosperity transcend all literal comprehension. What transfiguration will make the wolf lie down with the lamb—or men incapable of oppressing each other? Jewish thought moves between a "left-wing" view which sees the Messianic world as rid of tyrants only, and otherwise unchanged;[20] and a "right-wing" view which sees it apocalyptically transfigured.[21] But the mainstream of Jewish thought remains between these extremes.

The Messianic future, while the earliest eschatological expectation in Judaism, does not remain alone. Beside and beyond it emerges the hope for a "world-to-come" past all time and history. Although post-Biblical in origin, this has long been implicit in the Jewish faith,—ever since its God is believed to give meaning, wholly and in their own right, to individual lives. For whereas the Messianic future redeems an incomplete history, the world-to-come of eternity redeems the incomplete individual lives which exist in it.

Classical Jewish thought never achieves clarity as to the relation between these two expectations. This is inevitable. Not only is the world-to-come wholly past all finite understanding. Perhaps still more significantly, all attempts to reduce either of these dimensions to the other are consistently rejected, —at least until modernism makes some strains within Judaism doubt or reject life after death.

[20]Cf. e.g., the view of Maimonides, J. Klausner, *The Messianic Idea in Israel* (New York: Macmillan, 1955).

[21]Cf. e.g., the picture given in the so-called "Assumption of Moses," Klausner, *op. cit.*, p. 327.

First, orthodox post-Biblical theology quite deliberately embraces the belief in the world-to-come, despite its own orthodoxy and the absence of this belief from the Hebrew Bible.[22] The Divine commandment has accepted the individual; a Redemption would remain incomplete if it did not give him completion. But a Messianic end—by itself—would fail to do so, and indeed leave him a mere instrument of the historical process. The question asked by Jeremiah and Job is not answered by the historical process, even if complete.

No more can the Messianic goal of future time reduce itself to an Eternity beyond all time. A primordial Divine commanding Love has endowed history with meaning, in that it calls for meaningful human action. The great Divine-human drama of history thus initiated cannot be retroactively destroyed: by an end which makes this world a mere place in which to prepare for another, and in itself meaningless. Redemption must consummate both the history in which men work and wait, and the lives of the individuals who work and wait in it.

The two aspects of the eschatological expectation, then, remain mutually irreducible, and this despite the conscious recognition that Eternity must surely supersede all future history. This can be so because the world-to-come remains radically unintelligible. The rabbinic sources will say only that it will redeem the whole man whom the Divine commandment has accepted from the beginning,—not an immortal soul only but a resurrected psychosomatic totality;[23] and they are well aware that this is past all understanding. And they view silence on the subject as a necessity made obligatory by the Biblical silence which precedes it. "Rabbi Yohanan said: 'Every prophet prophesied only for the days of the Messiah; but as for the world-to-come, no eye has seen what God has prepared for those who wait for him'" (*RA.,* p. 598).

---

[22]It denies, however, its absence from the Bible (*RA.,* pp. 599, 607).

[23]Thus body and soul will both be judged on the day of last judgment (*RA.,* pp. 312 ff).

V. CHRISTIANITY

A CRISIS IN MEANING

In Samuel Beckett's play *Waiting for Godot* the central characters are two hobos, Estragon and Vladimir, who spend their time waiting for someone called Godot to turn up. They employ their days in an "aimless intensity" of passing the time, talking about nothing in particular. Estragon at one point sums up their predicament in his lament: "Nothing happens, nobody comes, nobody goes, it's awful!"[1]

To many people today life is "awful" because it appears to be nothing but "a tale told by an idiot," an endless procession of meaningless days, an "immense panorama of anarchy," or what T. S. Eliot terms "the void" with its "vacuum of disintegration."

Many writers claim that the chief anxiety of our time is that which is connected with the meaninglessness of existence. Life for millions can be described in Hobbes' words as "solitary poore, nasty, brutish, and short."

> One thing at least is certain—This life flies;
> One thing is certain and the rest is Lies;
> The flower that once is blown for ever dies.[2]

Life for many people adds up to zero. They look to the past and it seems to be a jumble of aimless events. They live in the present with its mad scramble for material security. They lift their gaze to the future—and all is dark. Where can life's meaning be found? would appear to be man's unspoken cry.

---

[1] *Modern Literature and the Religious Frontier*, Nathan A. Scott, Jr., (Quoted p. 86). (New York: Harper.)

[2] *The Rubaiyat of Omar Khayyam*, Second Edition, translated by Edward Fitzgerald, p. 31 (Everyman's Library).

Adam Schaff, professor of philosophy in Warsaw University and a noted Marxist, says that one day a student asked him in a seminar, "Could you explain the meaning of life, sir?" The professor took the question seriously. What actual reply he gave the student we do not know. However, the professor added that "as long as people die, suffer, lose their loved ones, just so long will questions about the meaning of life have full rights."[3]

Such a question must have "full rights" because it is the fundamental question of our human existence. Unless our religion has an adequate answer to give to this question about life's meaning we are left as very miserable creatures. We confront an "abyss" of nihilism. Or as some Existentialists would say, life is "absurd" and all of man's "blood, sweat and tears" comes to nothing. Man's life is "in vain." "Everything is tried and nothing satisfies."

Anatole France once wrote a story of a young king who, wishing to discover the lessons of history, appointed a commission of learned men to discover what these lesson are. In this story the author related that the last survivor of this commission, on his death-bed, whispered to the king the results of their labours: "Men are born, they suffer, they die: that is all." But if "that is all" there is to life many might be led to ask: is life worth living? For if "life is just a dirty trick," as a character in a modern novel states it is, then the sooner it ends the better for all concerned.

WHY IS LIFE MEANINGLESS FOR MANY?

Many reasons may be given, many critiques offered, to explain the widespread meaninglessness, the sense of futility and the incipient nihilism of our time. In this brief essay we can only mention a few of the causes which have brought about this

[3]*Time*, "A Red Morality?" June 2, 1961. P. 58.

modern malaise in the soul of man which has robbed him of life's purpose and goal.

First, there is the rise of science. Scientific development in recent decades has been a boon to man in many areas of his life. It has brought forth man's creative gifts. It has expanded the horizon of human existence. It has helped to stamp out some diseases, to lessen drudgery and pain, to hold out temporal hope for a better material existence for millions. Yet, on the other hand, man has tended to make science his god. He has come to regard it as the 'be-all and end-all" of life. He has become a devotee of science and the result is that his soul has become a "wasteland." "Man shall not live by bread alone" is an inescapable truth.

Secondly, there has appeared in our time a philosophy of secularism, of which Communism, economically and politically, and logical positivism philosophically, are two manifestations. This has been termed the first secular age in human history; that is, an age in which man has endeavoured to live on a social plane without any reference to a divine being or beings. To be secular in outlook means to be bounded by what is of the earth, earthy. This material universe is the sum and substance of existence for the secularist. His life is limited and circumscribed by the temporal and the material. He has no endless horizons of meaning; no ultimates on which he can build his life; no purpose around which to centre his aspirations.

Thirdly, the modern period of western history has tended to direct man's attention to man. This has brought about an irreligious humanism in which man and not God has become the focus of man's existence. Consequently man, who was made in the divine image according to Christianity, has "unmanned himself." He has severed his connection with the "ground of being" and he has become fretful in a lonely universe. Paul Tillich writes that "the anxiety of meaninglessness is anxiety about the loss of an ultimate concern, of a meaning which gives meaning to all meanings. This anxiety is aroused by the loss of a spiritual centre, of an answer, however symbolic and indirect, to the question of the meaning of existence. . . . The anxiety of emptiness drives us to the abyss of meaninglessness."[4] And this has come about because man has come to place himself at the centre of his universe instead of God.

It was the late William Temple who pointed out that the modern period began when René Descartes spent a day "shut up alone in a stove" and gave man the statement which might be taken as the basic text of our era: "I think, therefore I am" (*Cogito ergo sum*). But, as Temple points out, it is not "I" who is the centre of reference but God. God is of ultimate concern.[5]

Fourthly, uncertainty in matters of faith has arisen out of the cross-fertilization of cultures. Modern means of communication have made this "one world." We can no longer live in peaceful isolation. Ideas and customs from other lands and peoples have upset some of our "safe" standards. We no longer have the feeling of security which comes from an unchallenged faith. Many people, in consequence, find it difficult if not impossible to discover any of "the durable satisfactions of life."

Other reasons might be given as to why man today faces an "abyss of meaninglessness," such as insecurity in this atomic age, the rise of world Communism and its threat to freedom, the complexity of modern living, the intimidating vastness of the universe as made known by modern astronomy—and all these have had a part to play in the present predicament of man regarding a worthy purpose for his life. But we believe that basically man's life seems without meaning and purpose because he is out of touch with the spiritual centre of his life and his world. Man is a "lost" soul because he has lost God.

---

[4] *The Courage to Be,* Paul Tillich. P. 44f. (London: Nisbet & Co., Ltd.)

[5] *Nature, Man and God,* William Temple. P. 57 (New York: Macmillan).

The Secretary of State for the United States, Dean Rusk, is quoted as stating: "If war should break out . . . the Northern Hemisphere will simply be burned up. That means that Kennedy and Khrushchev both live with the first question of the Westminster (Shorter) Catechism always in mind: What is the chief end of man?"[6]

We believe as Christians that it is in the reply given to this question in the Westminster Shorter Catechism that we find the key to life's meaning and purpose. That reply is: "Man's chief end is to glorify God and enjoy him forever." All that any Christian can say about life's meaning and purpose will be by way of explication and elaboration of that famous answer. Job asks: "But where shall wisdom be found? and where is the place of understanding?" and gives reply: "Behold, the fear of the Lord, that is wisdom; and to depart from evil is understanding" (Job 28: 12, 28).*

Because God is the source of wisdom about life's meaning and purpose we must recognize that man's chief end is not in himself or from himself. His goal for living is in God and is given to him by God. The purpose of life, therefore, is something revealed to man, not something conceived by man's intellect. Man is able to discover life's purpose when he has the gift of faith. He can apprehend the meaning of his existence when he has first been laid hold of by God. He is given insight about the chief end of human living when God makes a divine disclosure about his own nature and purpose. In other words, man's purpose for living can only be known when it is seen to be part of God's purpose for the world. Man of himself, separated from his Creator, lives in the darkness of meaninglessness. Man living by faith in his Creator walks in the light of God's purpose and does not stumble and fall into the chasm of nihilism.

---

[6] *Life*, "Does He Drive or Is He Driven?" June 8, 1962. P. 84.
*All quotations from the Bible are from the Revised Standard Version.

What is God's purpose for the world? It may be stated in the words of St. Paul: "For he (Christ) has made known unto us in all wisdom and insight the mystery of his will, according to his purpose which he set forth in Christ as a plan for the fulness of time, to unite all things in him, things in heaven and things on earth" (Eph. 1 : 9, 10). Thus unity with God through Christ is the purpose of creation as set forth by the divine Creator. Man will find life's meaning and purpose, therefore, by identifying himself with this divine purpose and by realizing that he is a part of this universal plan. Or, to quote St. Paul again, "the eternal purpose which he has realized in Christ Jesus our Lord" . . . is that we might come "to know the love of Christ which surpasses knowledge, that you may be filled with all the fulness of God" (Eph. 3 : 11, 19).

Consequently, it is the individual who has faith in Jesus Christ, who accepts him as Lord and Saviour, who looks to him as the revealer of the divine will and purpose, who can discern God's plan for his creation and who can comprehend with all saints his own part in the eternal purpose of God. From the Christian standpoint it is utter nonsense to think that a secularist or an agnostic can come to know what the meaning and purpose of life is according to Christianity. Spiritual things are spiritually discerned. It is only by faith in him who gives light on life's meaning that we can understand the majestic will of God for man. In his light we shall see light.

Because faith is the key that unlocks the door to life's meaning and purpose we do not imply that it cannot be elucidated, or that the end of life according to Christianity cannot be set forth for others to know. Faith is not blind credulity. Nor is faith a contradiction of reason. Rather, faith is "reason grown courageous." Faith in the Christian sense of this term is seeing life under the aspect of Christ. Faith is personal trust in the Lord. This does not involve the renunciation of the intellect but its sanctification.

What, then, does faith in Jesus Christ disclose about God and his meaning and purpose for life?

First, by means of his revelation God has made known to us in Christ that we live in a world of order. St. Augustine said that order was the first law of God's universe. Some writers have stated that this belief in an orderly world, sustained by one God, has been one of the cornerstones in the development of modern science. It has given scientists a belief in the reliability and dependability of the world and its workings.

Some people, looking at the orderliness of creation, may say that it is the working of blind forces in a mechanical manner. But to the believer in Christ, the Word by whom the worlds were framed, this "mechanism" of nature reveals the orderly working of God's universe, the sort of thing we would expect in a world governed by a moral God whose nature and will are disclosed to us in the Man from Nazareth.

Moreover, this order in the world—the regularity of the seasons, the rising and setting of the sun, the "balance of nature" in the animal world, and many other observed phenomena—all points to some design. But how can one talk of order without an orderer, or design apart from a designer? And how can we speak of an orderer or designer except in terms of mind and purpose? When we look at the whole story of organic evolution from the biological standpoint alone, and consider the immensity of what appears to be a "plan," tending upward to man, it is impossible for one who has religious faith to omit God from this biological development, with its many new emergents, or exclude him from this order of a purposeful creation. It is faith in such a divine purpose and Purposer which alone makes sense of this scheme of things. Any other view is meaningless.

Secondly, this world reveals an element of beauty which may be regarded as another aspect of this order and design about which we have been speaking. Beauty fills many souls "with the joy of elevated thoughts." They have glimpses of "something far more deeply interfused" in nature, namely, the sense of divine mystery which such beauty presents to the human eye.

Some will say that the beauty we see in the world is only subjective; that it has no objective reality. But beauty is something which can only be perceived by a mind and to the theist who believes in a Creator the beauty of nature can be explained as the work of God who rejoices in his Creation. It is in such a realm that the poets, and not the scientists, take over. It is in this world of beauty that they speak to us of a Divine Artist whose creation declares, "the Hand that made us is divine."

One reason why we can claim that there is objectivity to beauty is that it appears to us as a discovery rather than a human invention. It strikes us as something which lays claim to our souls instead of something which we sought to find. "He on whom Beauty has cast her spell is not his own master," wrote William Temple, "though in his bondage he finds freedom. He must listen and gaze till his release is given."[7]

Moreover, the fact that there are standards of beauty, so that we argue whether or not a scene is beautiful and compare it with other evidences of beauty, makes us realize that there is an element of objectivity with respect to beauty, else we are only talking about our likes and dislikes. But again, how can we speak of an objective element in the realm of Beauty without reference to a Divine Artist?

Further, to experience beauty, that "moment eternal" in the midst of time, is to recognize the presence of purpose. When a person is seized by the aesthetic quality of a painting or a land

[7]*Mens Creatrix,* William Temple. P. 128 (New York, Macmillan)

86

scape he finds a joy in his soul that is ineffable. If he is looking at a painting of a great master he comes to see the purpose of the master in giving the world this product of his genius. Is it not similar as one beholds beauty in nature? Is there not in the very fact of the appreciation of such beauty an apprehension of purpose and meaning, a meeting of mind and Mind? No mechanistic or accidental explanation will suffice to make clear to our understanding an experience of beauty. The world with all its beauty only makes sense when we assume the reality of a divine Mind who is the source and author of all beauty.

THE MORAL LAW

Thirdly, Christianity declares that God's purpose is grounded in the moral law. "Life means intensely and means good." We believe that such a declaration is, among other things, supported by the moral nature of man. He is a free being, albeit within limits, because he can make choices. But along with his sense of freedom there is also a sense of obligation. The "I ought" of conscience, the categorical imperative of the moral will, cannot be treated as illusion. The fact of guilt which is to be found in the lives of those who disobey this "ought" testifies to the reality of the command.

"This absolute moral law in man's mind," writes Lindsay Dewar, "is also powerfully experienced when it is disobeyed. Every person who is honest with himself knows something of the poignancy of the feeling of a violated conscience. No earthly medicine can soothe the pains which come from deliberate refusal to obey the voice of conscience. It is idle to tell a person suffering from these pains that it doesn't matter; that everybody acts in this way; that the consequences will not be very serious. He knows that he has betrayed the noblest part of his being, and that a traitor he must always be . . . An absolute moral law involves a Law-giver, and that Law-giver we call God."[8]

LIFE MEANS LOVE

Fourthly, according to Christianity the meaning of life is love. To live is to love. "All's law, yet all's love." Or, to quote Browning again, "The All-Great were the All-loving too." The Law will be a sting to our conscience when we disobey the moral order and prove traitor. It is divine love, however, which forgives our iniquity and leads us on the path of perfection. Order, design, beauty, moral goodness—they all point to a supreme Being whom we call God. But it is in and through love that the fulness of his nature is revealed.

"God is love" (1 John 4: 8). This tremendous affirmation of the Christian faith is the basis of our belief that love is the law of life and that in and through love man finds the meaning and purpose of life. "God is love; and he who abides in love abides in God, and God abides in him" (1 John 4: 16). Here again we declare that all love that is worthy of the name is not a product of human devising but a revelation of God to man, a love which man apprehends by faith and expresses through the life of love. "If we love one another, God abides in us, and his love is perfected in us" (1 John 4: 12).

"God! Thou art love! I build my faith on that!"

(Paracelsus)

These words of Robert Browning can be said to be true for any genuine Christian. Apart from love, life is unintelligible. It is

> Only a scene
> Of degradation, ugliness and tears,
> The record of disgrace best forgotten.
> A sullen page in human chronicles
> Fit to erase.

(Paracelsus)

---

[8]*What Is the Purpose of Life?* Lindsay Dewar. P. 42 (London Rich and Cowan).

Only through love, God's love, can man find the meaning
and purpose of life.

> For life, with all its yields of joy and woe,
> And hope and fear—believe the aged friend—
> Is just our chance o' the prize of learning love,
> How love might be, hath been indeed and is.

> (*A Death in the Desert,* R. BROWNING)

The Christian maintains that it is love that gives life its
true purpose and worth. But we can only discern this worth
as we believe that love reigns supreme on the throne of the
universe, that God's name and nature is love.

THE FACT OF EVIL

But when we speak about God being good and loving in his
nature and his will we are confronted by the paradox of evil
in his world. If God is supreme and loving why is there evil?
Can a good God permit pain in his creation? How can we
justify the ways of God to man? "My God, my God, why?"
is the cry of the human heart in the face of suffering.

In reply we ought to state at the outset that there is no
intellectual solution of the problem of evil imparted by the
Christian faith. We must acknowledge "the mystery of iniquity."
Christianity instead of solving this problem offers victory over
evil. Christian belief does not eradicate suffering but it grants
people the spirit with which to conquer it.

There are some points which we may note as we confront
evil in all its forms. First, it is Christianity which makes this
question of the presence of evil in God's world all the more
serious because it says God is love. If we did not believe in a
loving Father the problem would not be nearly so difficult. But
when we say that God is love then the question arises in a very

acute form: Why does such a God allow his righteous ones to suffer?

Secondly, part of the problem can be seen in what has been called "the dread gift of free-will." God's purpose for man was to create a free and responsible creature who in moral love could respond to his divine mercy. In order to do this man must be free because only a person who is free can be moral. But such freedom involves the possibility of man saying "No" as well as "Yes" to God. And when man says "No" to his Maker he sins; he comes short of his glory. And it is sin, or moral evil, which is at the very heart of the problem of evil.

> Man's inhumanity to man
> Makes countless thousands mourn.

Thirdly, in order to develop a strong responsible character we must have something to struggle against, something that acts as a test of the soul. We are made perfect through suffering. Without struggle there would be no growth or development of character. Without pain there could be no gain. The life of ease and comfort leads to personal degeneration.

Thus the possibility of evil in our world may be looked upon as one source of man's distinctive excellence. There is, as Josiah Royce said, "the soul of good in things evil." This does not mean that evil is good in itself. It is not. But evil can be regarded as a steppingstone to the nobler life. The victory of the spirit through faith implies an antagonist, an adversary, and such a victory produces the character that is truly Christian. The saints of the Church have come to their saintliness through "peril, toil and pain." They have overcome the world of evil by trusting in the goodness of God. God is not the author of evil. Therefore, Christianity opposes evil in every form because it can have no part in the Kingdom of God and his realm of love. God, too, by his grace is overcoming evil. We believe that at the "end" he "must reign" and all evil be cast down forever. Then God and his love will be "all in all."

Discussion about God's love can be very abstract until we see his love incarnate. Christianity declares that "the Word became flesh and dwelt among us, full of grace and truth . . . No one has ever seen God; the only Son, who is in the bosom of the Father, he has made him known" (John 1: 14, 18). "God was in Christ," writes St. Paul, "reconciling the world to himself" (2 Cor. 5: 19).

In the New Testament it is apparent that when the early Christians thought of God's love they thought immediately of Christ and his Cross. "Thou must love me who hast died for thee." "In this the love of God was made manifest among us, that God sent his only Son into the world, so that we might live through him. In this is love, not that we loved God but that he loved us and sent his Son to be the expiation for our sins. Beloved, if God so loved us, we also ought to love one another" (1 John 4: 10, 11). The measure of God's love for men is that "Christ died for the ungodly" (Rom. 5: 6). "God shows his love for us in that while we were yet sinners Christ died for us" (Rom. 5: 8). The Cross is the proof of God's love. He loves each one of us as if there were but one of us to love, St. Augustine said. And he loves us like that! Calvary is the evidence of God's love for us.

It is in and through this love revealed in Jesus Christ that we come to know the meaning and purpose of life. "Life means Christ to me" (Phil. 1: 21, Moffatt), wrote St. Paul. "Life is meeting," as Buber says. This must first be a meeting with God in Christ and then a meeting with our brethren in him. "No man has ever seen God; if we love one another, God abides in us and his love is perfected in us" (1 John 4: 12). In Christ we see the meaning of life.

St. Paul sets forth the ingredients in the life of Christian love. "Love is patient and kind; love is not jealous or boastful; it is not arrogant or rude. Love does not insist on its own way; it is not irritable or resentful; it does not rejoice at wrong, but rejoices in the right. Love bears all things, believes all things, hopes all things, endures all things. Love never ends . . ." (1 Cor. 13: 4-8). It has been said that Jesus Christ sat for the portrait which St. Paul has painted in these lines. Instead of love we can insert the name Christ. He is the One who gives meaning to the term love.

Since Christians must interpret love in terms of Christ and his self-giving on the Cross the only sort of love about which we are entitled to speak in a Christian context is that of sacrificial love. This is not a matter primarily of the emotions but of the will. Christian love is the will to do good to others in spite of what they are and how they act. It is the will to love others unselfishly because God loves them. And in Christ he has gone all the way to exhibit his love, even to the Cross.

Would I suffer for him that I love? So wouldst thou—so wilt thou!
So shall crown thee the topmost, ineffablest, uttermost crown—
And thy love fill infinitude wholly, nor leave up nor down
One spot for the creature to stand in! It is by no breath,
Turn of eye, wave of hand, that salvation joins issue with death!
As thy Love is discovered almighty, almighty be proved
Thy power, that exists with and for it, of being Beloved!
He who did most, shall bear most; the strongest shall stand the most
    weak.
'Tis the weakness in strength, that I cry for! my flesh, that I seek
In the Godhead! I seek and I find it. O Saul, it shall be
A Face like my face that receives thee; a Man like to me,
Thou shalt love and be loved by, for ever: a Hand like this hand
Shall throw open the gates of new life to thee! See the Christ stand!

(From Saul, by R. Browning)

We have seen that Christianity proclaims that the meaning and purpose of life is to be found in love, the love of God which was incarnate in Jesus Christ the Lord and Saviour.

This love is revealed to us. It is not something which man can produce by his own volition. How, then, can man personally know this love of God which passes knowledge?

First, he must have faith in God through Jesus Christ. We have been speaking about faith by which we mean chiefly trust in the divine Father whose nature and will are made known to us in Christ. While such faith has an intellectual element which we term belief, nevertheless its predominant meaning is that of loyal commitment to a person, not to a set of propositions or teachings. "I live by faith in the Son of God, who loved me and gave himself for me," wrote St. Paul (Gal. 2: 20) out of his own personal experience. Such faith is not first of all a dogma or doctrine. It is an "I-Thou" encounter between man and God. Christ gives himself through faith. It is for Christians to discern the doctrine.

While faith is a matter of human response we must acknowledge that it is initiated by the grace of God. Faith is the offspring of grace. By God's grace we mean his undeserved love for the unworthy, unmerited and free. Divine grace is God's love coming to each of us in Chist, wherever we are, in order to redeem us unto himself. In such redemption we find life's meaning and purpose.

Faith also implies that man will repent of his sin and turn to God. Repentance is a turning away from all iniquity and a turning toward him Who is the "author and finisher of our faith." It means godly sorrow for past misdeeds and the wrong that has been harboured in the heart. Even more it involves an embracing of God's love in Christ, a willingness to enter into his realm of peace and joy and newness of life. In such a realm here and now man knows the meaning and purpose of his existence.

Secondly, we come to know the love of God which alone makes life worth living when we give him the obedience of our souls. Obedience is the organ of spiritual truth. Dedication

93

is the path that leads to life's design. "Walk while you have the light, lest darkness overtake you; he who walks in the darkness does not know where he goes. While you have the light, believe in the light, that you may become sons of light" (John 12: 35, 36).

The English words discipline and disciples come from the same root. A disciple of Christ must be a disciplined person in Christ. He is no longer one who can live according to the whims of the moment. He must obey the will of his Lord. He is a man under authority who gives allegiance to his supreme Commander. He obeys the commandments of the King of Kings and Lord of Lords. His discipleship commits him to One in whose service he finds perfect freedom.

> Make me a captive, Lord
> And then I shall be free;
> Force me to render up my sword,
> And I shall conqueror be.

This is the paradox of the Christian's life. In the surrender of joyful obedience the disciple finds the secret of life and the purpose of his existence.

Such obedience to Christ must be expressed in the service of love. "You shall love the Lord your God . . . and your neighbour as yourself" (Lk. 10: 27) is the supreme command given by Jesus to his followers. It is a divine imperative. "A new commandment I give to you, that you love one another; even as I have loved you, that you also love one another. By this all men will know that you are my disciples, if you have love one for another" (John 13: 34, 35). These words of Jesus to his disciples find support in the First Epistle of John: "If any one says, 'I love God', and hates his brother, he is a liar; for he who does not love his brother whom he has seen, cannot love God whom he has not seen. And this commandment we have from him, that he who loves God should love his brother also" (1 John 4: 20, 21).

94

Thirdly, we can come to know the meaning and purpose of life through God's love in Christ when we worship him in Christ's Name. The chief end of man is to glorify God and one of the ways in which we glorify him is through worship.

All life can be summed up in worship. It is man's total response to God's love in Christ. It is life's fulfilment, life's completion. It is the avenue to the beatific vision. It is in worship that we behold the mystery of eternity in this world of time and we become lost "in wonder love and praise" before the majesty of his cross and the breadth of his compassion toward us, the sinful sons of men.

A man's life is conditioned by what or whom he worships. According to his worship so will be his life. While worship is an end in itself, nevertheless it is through worship that our hearts are cleansed by God's holiness, our minds are informed by his truth, our wills strengthened by his purpose, and our souls inspired by his love. Worship in the Christian sense gathers up into itself all appreciation and gratitude so that we feel that

> Love so amazing, so divine,
> Demands my soul, my life, my all.

Moreover, Christian worship must always be inspired by that most selfless of all emotions, adoration. To come before God in Christ's Name is to adore and praise and magnify his holy name. It is in and through such adoration that in some mysterious way life's meaning and purpose are made plain to us and we know him, whom to know is life eternal.

Man's profound questions may be expressed in three words: whence? why? whither? Philosophers and sages in every age have endeavoured to answer the questions about man's life which are raised by these words. Many replies have been given, and not without some measure of wisdom. But the full answers to these questions cannot be found by the intellect alone. They can only be known in the depth of the human soul, where man communes through worship with his Maker, where soul meets Soul, and man knows that all is well. Such worship is an experience in which man enters into fellowship with his divine Lord and he "becomes breathless with adoration." "One fine hour" of genuine worship in Christ's name may be enough to open new horizons and help men to know that through the praise of God, life's clouds are dispersed, life's evils are overcome, and life's purpose is known by the adoring soul.

THE CHURCH

Having written about faith and repentance, obedience and worship, we must remember that in Christianity these are not carried out in isolation. Christians do not believe that genuine religion consists in "the flight of the alone to the Alone," as Plotinus described it. The Christian religion finds its beginning and end in the fellowship, that is in the Church, Christ's body, where faith is nurtured and men are led to repent of their sins; where obedience to God's will is enjoined and where God is worshipped in spirit and in truth. Apart from the community of the Church most of what we have been saying about life's meaning has little reality. The very fact that love is the law of life for Christians implies fellowship among our Lord's followers. Unity, as we have seen, is the very hallmark of God's purpose for man. And his Church is the instrument of this purpose, the medium through which God is working out his will to bring all men into communion with him in his Kingdom. Without the Church, we believe, God will not bring his purpose to completion and apart from his Church man will not be able to find the meaning of life. God's love is known only in fellowship.

While the Church is a necessary instrument for fulfilling God's will in this world, we do not think of it as a perfect institution, or a fellowship of people without error or sin. Rather the Church is the community of forgiven sinners who know they are sinful and seek for divine grace. They realize they are not good in themselves and they need the goodness of God.

The Church being Christ's body has a universal responsibility. It is not a limited liability corporation. Its work is not confined to any one land or continent. All creatures of the Creator belong within the concern of the Church. Toward them the Church has a duty under God to call men everywhere to the worship of God in Christ, to proclaim the good news of the Gospel, to minister to human need in every form wherever it may be, to oppose evil and pronounce upon it the judgment of God, and to be a reconciling agency in the world. Such a responsibility must be exercised in both the spiritual and material realms of life, since God is the Lord of both the invisible and visible worlds. The Church believes, therefore, that this task committed to it by its Lord must be undertaken with a sense of accountability to him who is the Head of the Body, even Jesus Christ.

Further, in its prophetic task of pronouncing the moral will of God on national and international relationships the Church believes that it is called to do this because the judgments of God are in the whole earth. No people are exempt from the divine law. The world is built on moral foundations and the Church is constrained by its faith to say to all men, "This is the way. Walk in it" (Is. 30: 21)!

From the standpoint of the Christian faith, therefore, the fulness of life's meaning and purpose cannot be realized without the Church. It is the community of the risen Saviour and consequently the fellowship of faith and hope and love.

Furthermore, because of the nature of God's purpose in which we are called to participate, human history also has meaning through Christ. The Lord whom we Christians worship is the cosmic Christ. He is not merely Lord in his Church. He is also Lord in the world. "He is the image of the invisible God, the first-born of all creation; for in him all things were created, in heaven and on earth, visible and invisible, whether thrones or dominions or principalities or authorities—all things were created through him and for him. He is before all things, and in him all things hold together" (Col. 1: 15-17).

This belief that God is the Lord of creation implies that history is the arena in which God is working out his purpose of love. The events of the generations are not a meaningless string of occurrences. They are the very stuff in which God is endeavouring to unite all things in Christ. History is his story. Here in this human scene of time God is making his will known to men.

In the ancient world, in contrast to this Christian belief, there was held a cyclical view of history which represented all human events occurring in endless cycles. There was no creating God in control of the world, so it was said. Nothing new or unique could happen according to this point of view. Man was a helpless victim on the wheel of existence. Originality and creativity were impossible in this philosophy.

All this was changed by Christianity. The Gospel declared that history was moving toward a goal—the Kingdom of God. The meaning of this goal had already appeared in history in the person of Jesus Christ. He was the new centre of history who gave meaning to all that preceded his coming and who shed light on all that had happened since a Star shone over Bethlehem on the first Christmas.

Because of this faith in Christ as the Lord of History Christians see that even as he came into history to redeem it, so God in Christ is still seeking through the Holy Spirit to work out his purpose of love on this human plane and ultimately bring the Kingdom to completion and fulfilment. God is, therefore, present today in history, ruling it providentially and purposefully, and by his divine alchemy transforming the contingencies of history into agencies of his will.

It is part of the Christian faith that God came into history in the person of Christ who has now ascended to heaven, but who will return to gather all things to himself and create "a new heaven and a new earth." In this strong symbolism of the Second Coming of Christ we have the affirmation of the triumph of God over all evil. This victory of Christ and his Kingdom will not bring about the annulment or annihilation of history, but its transformation.

Christianity is an eschatological religion. Its faith is rooted in an eternal world. But it believes that God has manifested himself in this world of time and space, thereby giving meaning and purpose to all that happens in this earthly scene of things. In and through Christ and his message history has eternal significance.

It may be asked: where is history tending? Christianity replies: toward Christ and his Kingdom. In and through history's Lord we see that the lives of men and women, their struggles and achievements, come to fulfilment in that which is the goal of history, the consummation of the Kingdom.

THE CENTRALITY OF CHRIST

It must be apparent from what we have written that Christianity stands or falls with the person and work of Jesus Christ who is the revelation of God in time, the One through whom we can find the meaning and purpose of life. Christians believe that Jesus Christ is Lord of all, the One who makes real to us the nature of our heavenly Father. Christianity affirms that "there is salvation in no one else, for there is no other name under heaven given among men by which we must be saved" (Acts 4: 12). This is the truth which we derive from God's revelation of himself in him Who is the true and living Way. "Thanks be to God for his inexpressible gift" (2 Cor. 9: 15).

The import of what we have been writing in this essay about the unique claims that Christianity makes for its Lord is that there is an element of exclusiveness in the Christian faith. In one sense we must agree with such a statement. The Third Assembly of the World Council of Churches declared: "When we speak to men as Christians we must speak the truth of our faith: that there is only one way to the Father, namely, Jesus Christ his Son. On that way we are bound to meet our brother. We meet our brother Christian. We meet also our brother man; and before we speak to him of Christ, Christ has already sought him."[9]

Christianity, however, is exclusive in its claims not for itself or for the Church and its forms of religious expression, but for its Lord. He is the one Mediator between God and man. To believe that there are other lords who can take his place, or to reduce him to the category of a religious leader, is to deny the central tenet of the Christian faith, namely, that he is the world's redeemer and there is no other.

Moreover, Christianity is exclusive in the sense that it does not permit its followers to amalgamate its faith with those of other religions. One reason for this is that many Christian beliefs are incompatible with beliefs in other faiths. How, for example, can we unite belief in God who is working out his purpose in history with a faith which holds that history is illusion? Or how can we link the Christian doctrine of sin and salvation with a religion which does not hold to a belief in either sin or salvation?

Further, and contrary to other religions, Christianity places the teachings of Christ as secondary in importance to Christ himself. He, and not his teachings, are central in the faith.

---

[9]*The New Delhi Report,* p. 321 (S.C.M.).

He is the Event by which all other events are judged. He is the watershed of time, the focus of meaning in history. To him and to none other we must commit the total allegiance of our souls.

THE UNIVERSAL CHRIST

While Christianity is exclusive in its claims for Christ, at the same time it is also inclusive. "God so loved the world" (John 3: 16). The Christian gospel has a world view. "There is neither Jew nor Greek, there is neither slave nor free, there is neither male nor female; for you are all one in Christ Jesus" (Gal. 3: 28).

This inclusive or universal element in the gospel, coupled with the divine urgency and constraint in its proclamation of the love of God, has made Christianity from the beginning a missionary faith. Like Peter and John, the Church throughout the ages has declared: "We cannot but speak of what we have seen and heard" (Acts 4: 20). Christians believe that in Jesus Christ God has come to redeem his people, to gather together from every kindred and tongue and nation those who accept him as Lord.

This does not mean that Christians have any sense of superiority over other men. We can readily acknowledge, for example, the moral excellence of a man like M. Gandhi. Rather, Christians must witness to Christ in humility because they realize their own unworthiness. Moreover, Christians feel at one with all men because, like all men, they are sinners. Christians testify not of themselves but of their Lord who has saved them from the power and guilt of sin and has reconciled them to the Father.

Either Jesus Christ was what he claimed to be and what the Church has always called him, "The Light of the World," or else he is the greatest impostor who ever lived. There is no half-way house in which we can live when we face the question:

101

"What think ye of Christ?" Christians believe that Christ is the truth. In the light of this affirmation the question as to whether one religion is better than another has no significance. Christ is the incomparable Lord. If, as we believe, he has the secret of eternal life, the Church has the clear responsibility placed upon it by God to declare this truth to all men.

This does not mean that the Church is "going out to enrol men under the banner of a tribal deity. We are not inviting strangers to come into our house. We are asking all men to come to their own home where they have as much right as we have . . . Christ belongs now as truly to the Hindu and the Muslim as he does to us. He is now their true light. He is not the head of religion, but the head and King of the human race."[10]

Bishop Stephen Neill believes there should be more dialogue between Christians and Hindus and Muslims, for example. But he says we must never try to state the Christian faith in such general terms that we have nothing specific and challenging to present to men. He lists seven basic convictions which he says the Church must always maintain if its witness is to remain within the Christian sphere. These are:

1. There is only one God and Creator, from whom all things take their orgin.
2. This God is a self-revealing God, and he himself is active in the knowledge that we have of him.
3. In Jesus the full meaning of the life of man, and of the purpose of God for the universe, has been made known In him the alienated world has been reconciled to God.
4. In Jesus Christians see the way in which they ought to live his life is the norm to which they are unconditionally bound
5. The Cross of Jesus shows that to follow his way will certainly result in suffering; this is neither to be resented nor to be avoided.

---

[10]*A Faith for This One World?* Lesslie Newbigin. P. 65f (London S.C.M. Press).

6. The Christian faith may learn much from other faiths; but it is universal in its claims; in the end Christ must be acknowledged as Lord of all.

7. The death of the body is not the end. Christ has revealed the eternal dimensions as the true home of man's spirit.[11]

THE CHURCH'S DUTY AND AUTHORITY

We believe that all men are made in the image of God. This is the first bond of our common humanity. But man by his sin has marred this image. He has perverted and corrupted his true nature. He has sinned and consequently he is in need of redemption. Further, we believe that it is at the cross of Jesus Christ that the heinousness of man's sin and rebellion are brought home to us. But at the cross we also know of that divine love which overcomes our sin, which pardons our transgressions and which makes us new creatures in Christ Jesus. Because of such beliefs, which are based on the unique events in the ministry of Jesus Christ, crucified, risen, and ascended— events which are without parallel—the Church has always felt compelled to go and tell others that they, too, may believe and find salvation in him. "Our duty and authority to preach the gospel to all men," writes Lesslie Newbigin, "rest upon the fact that God has provided in Christ Jesus one mercy-seat where man's total rebellion is judged and pardoned. Our task is to bring all men to that place. There is no room here for comparing ourselves with others—either to our own advantage or to theirs. Judgment belongs to God. Our business is to bring all men to the one place where the judge has come to meet us all in order to have mercy upon us all."[12]

It comes to this. The Church has no alternative. If she is to be the Church, Christ's body, she must go forth into all the

---

[11] *Christian Faith and Other Faiths,* Stephen Neill. P. 229f. (Oxford)
[12] *Op. cit.* p. 77.

world under the banner of the cross and declare, "By this sign conquer!" To withhold her witness to the Lordship of Jesus Christ and to take the attitude that faith in him is no longer a question of life or death; to imply by words or by indifference that it does not matter what a man believes; to teach that Christ's Lordship is not unique or essential for salvation is to elect to become something other than the Church which we find in the New Testament.

The Church has been put in trust with the gospel. She has been commissioned by her Lord to take this gospel to earth's remotest parts. She must remain faithful to her trust in this decisive hour in human history. "In his will is our peace."

M. RASJIDI

(Assisted by J. B. Hardie)

VI. ISLAM

Islam is primarily a religion. It may by its very nature take the form of a state, or even of an empire; it may express itself in social and economic forms; but it is first and foremost a relationship between God and man.

It is therefore in the light of this relationship that the meaning of human life is to be seen. And in order to understand the basic principles of the Islamic philosophy of life it is necessary to go back, as many modern Muslims are doing, to the first development of the religion.

Like all faiths, Islam has had its fluctuations between strength and weakness. Like the rest it has known ages when its practice was by no means equal to its profession. It is therefore wrong to assess it by reference to any one period or locality, to any one group of Muslims in its later history. As a religion grounded in history, and with a revealed Scripture, it can be properly understood only by reference to the age and the circumstances in which it originated.

Islam is the religion preached in the Arabian Peninsula at the beginning of the seventh century of the Christian era by the Prophet Muhammad, whose life and experience are inextricably woven into the history of the religion.

Born about A.D. 570 into the influential tribe of Quraish in Mecca, Muhammad at the age of forty became conscious of a prophetic call. Under the guidance of successive revelations he began to preach in Mecca against the heathenism of Arabia. He proclaimed the existence of One God, Allah, who calls men to repentance and submission, and who gives to Muhammad the Arabic Qur'an for the guidance of mankind.

This preaching proved unpopular at Mecca, and Muhammad

105

and his few adherents had to suffer considerable persecution and hardship. At one point this became so intense that the Prophet sanctioned the departure of some of his followers to take refuge in Christian Abyssinia. He never faltered, however, in his religious convictions or in his faith that ultimately Islam would be the religion of all Arabia.

The Prophet's fortunes changed for the better when, after some ten years of preaching at Mecca, he accepted the invitation of some of the inhabitants of the neighbouring city of Yathrib to migrate thither. This event is known as the *Hijra,* or emigration, and from it the Muslim calendar still dates. The identification of Muhammad with his new headquarters is fitly evidenced by the fact that henceforth the city is known, not as Yathrib, but as Madinat an-Nabi, the City of the Prophet, or more commonly Medina.

In Medina Islam first took on its characteristic aspect; it was established not only as a religion but also as a form of society and as a state, with Muhammad at its head. Rejecting the idea of a priesthood in favour of a democratic religious equality, in which all believers stood on the same footing before God, the Prophet put the same principle into practice in his society. Thus, for example, he established "brotherhood covenants" between individuals from the *muhajirun,* the emigrants from Mecca, and the *ansar,* the Medinese "helpers," with such good effect that he welded potential rivals and enemies into one community, obedient to his will and fanatical for his cause.

This was the basis of his success. Despite continued opposition from Mecca, Muhammad finally returned to his native city as conqueror, and when he died in 11 A.H. all of Arabia was united for the first time in loyalty to Islam and to the Prophet of Allah.

Although the Prophet Muhammad is not the object of worship in Islam, as Jesus Christ is in Christianity, yet his character, his influence and his authority are indispensable factors in formulating any doctrine of the meaning of life in Islam.

This religion is not properly referred to as Muhammadanism, in spite of the popularity of this term in the West, because such a name implies for the man Muhammad a position of veneration which was neither claimed by himself nor accorded by his followers. The true position is indicated in the *shihada,* the Muslim profession of faith, with its two-fold assertion: I testify that there is no god but Allah; I testify that Muhammad is the Apostle of Allah.

The Arabic word *rasul,* together with its equivalents, *nabi,* a prophet, and *nazir,* a warner, is the title by which Muhammad goes in the Qur'an. And these terms make clear his function, which is that of a prophet in the true and original sense of prophecy, that of acting as the spokesman of God, as the bringer of a revelation given from on high. Thus in Qur. V: 70: "O Messenger, deliver that which has been sent down to thee from thy Lord; for if thou dost not, thou wilt not have delivered his message."

The message with which Muhammad was entrusted was the Qur'an, which was directly revealed to him by God on a variety of occasions. Sometimes it came like a dream so clear that it resembled the dawn, sometimes like a bell ringing in his ear; at other times an angel in the form of a human being came to him and taught him the verses. Such revelations came to him in an almost uninterrupted succession during a period of twenty-three years between his call to prophesy and his death, and since they were determinative for the faith and practice of the Muslim community they were preserved both by writing and by memorization on the part of the Companions.

As time went on, the Companions of the Prophet, the first generation of Muslims, were taken away not only by the natural course of events but even more by the hard course of battles in which Islam was involved. Accordingly Abu Bakr, the first Caliph, had a collection made of all the Qur'anic materials by Zaid ibn Thabit, the official secretary of the Prophet, who might therefore be reasonably supposed to have the most complete knowledge of the revelations.

This collection was preserved by Abu Bakr, and after his death by Umar, the second Caliph, who entrusted it to the care of his daughter Hafsa, one of Muhammad's widows.

But a new danger soon became apparent. Despite the casualties, there were still many of the Companions who remembered the Prophet's oracles, and as these followed the Muslim conquests into ever more remote countries their memories of what Muhammad had actually said began to differ in greater or lesser degree.

In order to meet this difficulty Uthman, the third Caliph in line from the Prophet, ordered the compilation of an authoritative Qur'anic text from the materials available in the house of Hafsa. Copies of this were sent to all the principal Muslim capitals, while a master copy was retained at Medina, the official centre of the Caliphate. It is this "authorized version" of Uthman which is to this day the only official text of the Qur'an.

In the Qur'an, therefore, Islam possesses a positive, historical revelation, which is its primary ground of authority for life and religion. This may be supplemented, as we shall see, by reference to the *Sunna,* or custom of the Prophet, and to the *Hadith,* or tradition literature handed down on the authority of the Companions of the Prophet; but the real basis of Muslim faith and practice is the "positive, historical revelation" embodied in the Qur'an.

Each of these three words demands separate consideration, if we are fully to understand the Qur'an and its importance.

In the first place, it is "revelation." The message which Muhammad proclaimed, and which became the Qur'an, was not his own, but God's.

This is made clear in many places, but above all in the first revelation which the Prophet received in the cave on Mount Hira. It is now contained in Sura XCVI: 1-5, which runs thus: "Read, by the name of your God, who created man from a clot of blood, read! Your God is the most venerated, who taught by the pen, teaching man what he does not know yet." The important word here is the verb "read", in Arabic *qara'a*; it means to read aloud or proclaim, and from it is derived the name Qur'an itself. Muhammad, that is to say, does not compose the content of his preaching; he is to read aloud, or proclaim, that which is shown to him in his vision.

This idea of the Qur'an as something given from above is found repeatedly. For example, in Sura XLI: 1 we have: "A sending down from the Merciful, the Compassionate; a book whose signs are detailed; an Arabic Qur'an for a people having knowledge." It is something "sent down" from God for the guidance of men. Of this book Muhammad is only the mediator and the example of how its precepts are to be carried out (Sura XXXII: 21). At the centre of Islam therefore there stands a Divinely revealed Scripture, rather than a man.

Secondly, the Qur'an is historical. Its revelation, that is to say, took place under certain historical circumstances which can be determined, and through a person whose nature, character, actions and habits are recorded in detail. God's book did not come into a vacuum, but as the answer to certain ascertainable human situations and needs.

It is always essential that the Qur'an be understood against the background of its historical context, else there is grave danger of misinterpretation. For example, the reader will find that Sura IX: 4 reads as follows: "Then, when the sacred months are drawn away, slay the idolaters wherever you find them, and take and confine them, and lie in wait for them at every place of ambush." Without knowing that this was revealed in order to meet a certain historical situation in the Medinan period, the reader might be tempted to take it out of its context and interpret it as an indication of the aggressive nature of Islam—which is in reality quite contrary to Islam's principle of freedom in religion.

The first prerequisites, therefore, of an understanding of the Qur'an and its meaning for life are study and knowledge.

And these are underlined by the nature of the book in its present form. It consists of 6254 verses, which are arranged in 114 chapters or Suras varying in length from 286 long verses to 3 short. The arrangement is neither chronological nor by subject matter; chapters are composed as units for memorization and recitation, and may include a large number of topics— stories drawn from ancient history, warnings of the Day of Judgment, exhortation, legislation and so on.

Thirdly, the Qur'an is positive, in the sense that it has one definitive form. It is self-described as "an Arabic Qur'an," and hence it cannot in the view of many Muslims be properly translated. There is, as we have seen, only one text, and that text is for recitation aloud in Arabic, in which it has a sonorousness and a power which cannot be communicated through translation.

The power of Qur'anic recitation is well attested from the earliest times. Many of the Companions, for instance, owed their first conversion to hearing the Prophet recite his revelations, or to hearing these recited by others. Umar was one such. Although he himself was a formidable unbeliever, his sister embraced the new religion; in anger he punished her, but she remained steadfast in her faith, and in demonstration of it she recited some Qur'anic verses. On hearing them, Umar went at once to Muhammad and became a Muslim.

A somewhat similar story is related of Abu Bakr. Having himself become a Muslim, he used to recite the Qur'an in his yard, and so persuasive was the reading that many of the Meccans tended to be converted. This caused the unbelieving authorities of the city to prohibit the future Caliph from reading the Qur'an publicly, lest he attract even more of their numbers to his faith.

The Qur'an, therefore, as revealed in Arabic on certain historically identifiable occasions, forms the primary ground for an understanding of the Muslim view of life. But it may be supplemented from two other related sources already mentioned, the *Sunna* and the *Hadith*.

The former of these is the "custom" or habit of the Prophet

110

Muhammad. He is not in Islam the object of any "Muhammadology," but he is described in the Qur'an as an "example" to mankind, and therefore Muslim life and practice may be modelled on the manner in which he did things. Prayers, for example, are commanded in the Qur'an, but no specific instructions are to be found on how to pray, in what words and with what bodily movements. In such cases the Prophet is taken as the model, and his common practice is followed.

Allied to the *Sunna* is the body of literature known as the *Hadith* or tradition, which also depends on the authority of the Prophet. It comprises a carefully and critically selected corpus of sayings and incidents which are not contained in the Qur'an but which are reported of the Prophet on the unimpeachable authority of his Companions.

All of this serves to tie the whole Islamic system closely to history. It belongs to a precisely defined course of events, whose details and personalities are those of the Arabian Peninsula at the beginning of the seventh century of the Christian era, whose language is classical Arabic, and whose social and economic background are alike very different from those of the present.

But the very fact of this intimate connection with a certain historical setting may well serve to raise the question of the present-day relevance of Islam as a system of faith and life. How, it may be asked, can a religion which grew up in Arabia so many centuries ago be appropriate to the needs of urbanized mankind today? Or can a way of life so closely and characteristically Arab be appropriate to other countries and other times?

The answer to these and other similar questions can be supplied only by an understanding of what Islam is, as propounded in the Qur'an.

To begin with, the very fact that it is a revealed religion means that it is independent of time and space. It is the revelation (*wahy*) which God has "sent down" (*anzala*) to Muhammad, and as such it is timeless and changeless. Take, for instance, the great definition of religion in Sura II: 62, "Whosoever believe in God and the last day, and act righteously, their wage awaits them with their Lord, and no fear shall be on them, neither shall they sorrow." This is applied to Jews, Christians and Sabaeans, and not only to Muslims; but it states a principle of religion which is valid regardless of time, place or circumstance.

But this is by no means all. The Qur'an proclaims that Islam (meaning literally "submission" to the will of God) is no new religious system, but in fact the religion of Abraham. So, for example, in Sura III: 67, "Abraham in truth was not a Jew nor a Christian; but he was a Muslim and one pure of faith; certainly he was never of the idolaters."

Or again, in Sura XXII: 78, "And struggle for God, as is his due; for he has chosen you, and has laid on you no impediment in your religion, being the creed of your father Abraham. He named you Muslims aforetime and in this (book), that the Messenger might be a witness against you, and that you might be witnesses against mankind. So perform the prayers and pay the alms and hold you fast to God; he is your Protector, an excellent Protector and an excellent Helper."

Or finally, in Sura III: 83, "Say, we believe in God, and in that which has been sent down upon us, and sent down upon Abraham and Ishmael, Isaac and Jacob and the Tribes, and in that which was given to Moses and Jesus and the Prophets of the Lord. We make no division between any of them, and to him we are submissive (*muslimun*). Whosoever desires another religion than Islam, it shall not be accepted of him; in the next world he shall be among the losers."

This brings us to the question of the relation between Islam and the other, earlier religions. On this matter the Qur'an is specific: Islam is the peak of the religious systems of the world, just as Muhammad is "the Seal of the Prophets." God has sent at least one prophet to every people; the Qur'an contains the accounts of those which are familiar to Jews and Christians from the Bible, and also of others such as Hud and Salih.

Some of these peoples listened; some did not. "Indeed we sent forth among every nation a messenger saying: Serve your God and exclude idols. Then some of them God guided . . . and some were justly disposed to error." Muhammad is the last, the greatest, the "seal" (*khatim*) of the prophets, and his supreme sign or miracle is the Arabic Qur'an itself.

This means that Islam is not limited in its scope to the Arabs, to whom it was first declared. Muhammad is sent by God to deliver his message to all mankind. "I sent you as a Messenger to all human kind" (Sura IV: 78); "I sent you to all of the human kind as an announcer of good news and as a warner, but most of the human kind do not understand" (Sura XXXIV: 28). And the Prophet certainly took this office in all seriousness, as is shown by the fact that at one period of his mission he wrote formal letters to all the neighbouring rulers, including the Byzantine Emperor, the Persian Khosroes and the Christian Emperor of Abyssinia, inviting them to become Muslims.

But Islam's claim to relevance for today does not rest solely on its supernatural origin or its original claims to universality. It is a religion which welcomes, and even commands, the use of reason, knowledge and argument, such as are typical of the modern spirit.

Thus, for instance, Islam insists on the reasonableness (*aql*) of the universe as a reason for belief in God. One of the best-known verses of the Qur'an testifies to this:

> Surely in the creation of the heavens and the earth
>   In the alternation of day and night,
> In the ship which runs on the sea with profit to men,
>   In the water which God sends down from thence,
> Therewith reviving the earth after it is dead;
> In His scattering abroad in it all manners of crawling things;
>   In the turning about of the winds
> And the clouds compelled between heaven and earth—
> Surely these are signs for a people having reason.

> —(Sura II: 164)

Thus in Islam, as also in Christian Thomist theology, there are the two levels of religious knowledge—that which is "natural," the fruit of apprehension based on observation, and that which is "given," the revealed or supernatural. And correspondingly, the meaning of life for Islam is not to be interpreted simply and solely in terms of otherworldliness, or with reference only to a long past and gone set of historical and geographical circumstances. It is a philosophy which forms an integral part of the great universal scheme of Divine revelation; thus it finds the true meaning of human life only in relation to the God who created that life, and who sends down his commands for it. But the corresponding duty of man is not merely a credulous and unthinking acceptance of the incredible. It is rather to work through the application of his revealed faith to the realities of life as it exists in any and every age, in all countries and under all circumstances.

With these things in mind we may now turn to a more detailed examination of the Muslim's concept of the meaning of life. The question may be best approached from the point of view of man's dual nature—as an individual and as a member of society. These aspects are different, but they are interrelated. Man as an individual has a personal, inner life which is realized in communion with God, and which has certain inalienable, individual rights. But he is also a member of a community, of a race, in which his rights may be in some ways curtailed, in some ways fulfilled. And the meaning of human life can be expressed only by bringing these two aspects into harmony.

The keynote of man's inner or individual life in Islam is struck by the name of the religion itself. Islam is a verbal noun meaning submission or handing over; the Muslim as an individual is one who by a voluntary act of submission becomes the "slave of God." He worships him alone, he communicates directly with him through prayer, he fulfils his demands as these are revealed in the Qur'an, and he subordinates his own will to the Divine Will.

But there are also other meanings of the Arabic word which are not less significant. As is generally known, the related word Salaam is universally used in Muslim countries as a greeting, meaning Peace. It is by no means irrelevant to think of Islam as the religion of peace through submission, of that inner peace of mind and spirit which is achieved through the surrender of life to God.

Finally, the verb has the sense of being whole or complete, which may act as a fitting reminder that Islam thinks of human life as reaching its completion, its wholeness, only when it is set in the context of the greater life and the larger purpose which are found in God alone.

This submission to the Divine Will expresses itself in a variety of ways, which we shall consider here. But principally it may be thought of as man's understanding of his creatureliness, his humility in the face of his Creator, his utter dependance on God who is all-powerful.

This acceptance of the overwhelming power and majesty of God is the theological heart of Islam. But it does not mean, as has been so frequently represented in the Western world, that Muslims must believe in the kind of fatalism which robs human life of all real meaning, and which makes of men no more than puppets manipulated by the decrees of an inscrutable Deity.

The Qur'an certainly presents God as the almighty Lord of the worlds which he has created. There is no limit to his power, nor is there anything which can happen without being decreed by is will. So in XLII : 48-49, "To God belongs the sovereignty of the heavens and the earth. He createth what he pleaseth, giving to whom he pleaseth females and to whom he pleaseth males, or conjoining them males and females, and he maketh whom he pleaseth barren; verily he hath knowledge and power."

Or in LVII: 22-23, "No affliction befalls in the earth or in yourselves, but it is in a Book before we create it; that is easy for God; that you may not grieve for what escapes you, nor rejoice in what has come to you."

To this unqualified and unlimited power men are unquestionably subordinate. They can do nothing except as God wills it, at least in the sense of permitting it.

Yet this is only one side of the matter. For the Qur'an equally teaches a doctrine of human responsibility, under which all individuals must answer for their deeds to God who is the Lord of the Day of Judgment. This belief runs so deep in Islam that it is always quoted as one of the characteristic marks of the faith; but there would be no reason and no meaning in a Day of Judgment unless human beings were responsible for their actions. Words like sin and wrong-doing are devoid of meaning, cannot even be used, if man is simply the passive recipient of God's actions. Yet the Qur'an has much to say of them.

Take such a passage as Sura XVIII: 28-30. "And say: 'The truth is from your Lord; so who wills, let him believe, and who wills, let him disbelieve;' verily we have prepared for the wrong-doers a Fire . . . But those who have believed and done the works of righteousness—verily we do not allow to go to loss the reward of any who do well in deed. For them are Gardens of Eden."

The whole idea of reward and punishment which is so clearly stated here is obviously dependent on the theory that man is morally responsible for his actions. Even religious belief, as it is phrased in this passage, is the outcome of an act of the human will.

Similarly, among the most characteristic Qur'anic descriptions of God are the adjectives "the Merciful," "the Compassionate," "the Forgiving." For instance, in Sura XXXIX: 53: "Say: Oh my people who have been prodigal against yourselves, do not despair of God's mercy. Surely God forgives sins altogether. Surely he is the All-forgiving, the All-compassionate." But if man is merely the victim of a Divine predestination, then he can have no sins; and then God cannot be Forgiving, for he has nothing to forgive.

The whole pattern of life in Islam makes it abundantly

clear that the doctrine of Divine decree is not such as to preclude man's free will. Any extreme form of fatalism makes nonsense of "good works"; yet these form a major part of a Muslim's religious duties. This tension is already seen, even if it is not fully resolved, in the Qur'an itself. Sura XXXVI: 47 presents the extreme fatalistic position (which was characteristic of pre-Islamic Arabia) in blunt form, in the context of giving alms. "When one says to them, 'Contribute of what God hath provided you with,' the unbelievers say to the believers, 'Shall we feed him whom, if God so willed, he would feed? You are only in manifest error'."

This is the kind of predestination in which Islam does not believe. It can result only in apathy and irresponsibility. Worse —it must ultimately make human life meaningless.

The Muslim, then, believes in the subordination of the human will to the Divine Will; but that subordination is a self-conscious act, which calls for the disciplining of life.

This discipline, which is actually a spiritual process, has its counterpart in the physical life. Islam does not countenance asceticism as a normal rule of life; it has no doctrine of the essentially evil nature of the body or of the physical world. But it believes in bringing the body and its needs and demands into subjection. As everyone knows, the Qur'an prohibits the use of intoxicants, just as it forbids also the practice of the gambling game familiar to pre-Islamic Arabia as *al-maisar*— for basically the same reason, that these are indulgences of the body and the spirit which have no place in the disciplined life which man owes to his Creator.

But the disciplinary aspect of submission is perhaps best illustrated by the institution of fasting which is obligatory on all Muslims for one month each year. During the month of Ramadan from first light until sunset the Muslim is required to abstain from all indulgence of the flesh, including both food and drink. This is a severe enough test of physical and spiritual fortitude at any time; but the Muslim calendar follows a lunar system, and therefore every so many years Ramadan will fall in the height of the hot season. Fasting then becomes a real mortification of the flesh, but it is maintained as a reminder that man's natural and proper enjoyment of the world is subject to his obedience to his Creator.

The dependence of man upon God, which provides the context of Islam's view of the meaning of life, is further seen in the prayers (*salat*) which, like fasting, form one of the so-called "five pillars of Islam."

Five times every day the Islamic community is called to formal prayer, proclaimed from the minaret of the mosque by the muezzin in the time-honoured formula, "Come to prayer!" In the prayers every bodily motion, every gesture and every word testifies to man's humility in the presence of God. Here again, in the kneeling posture and the humble words there is further indication of the submission to a God who is always present with his human creatures.

This "practice of the presence of God" is often inculcated in the Qur'an, just as it is familiar to pious Muslims, not only through the statutory prayers but also in the dialogue with God which is the private exercise of the spirit.

So, for example, Sura LVIII: 7, "Hast thou not seen that God knows whatsoever is in the heavens and whatsoever is in the earth? Three men conspire not secretly together, but he is the fourth of them; neither five men, but he is the sixth of them; neither fewer than that nor more, but he is with them wherever they may be; then he shall tell them what they have done, on the Day of Resurrection. Surely God has knowledge of everything."

Or Sura II: 286, "Our Lord, take us not to task if we forget or make mistake. Our Lord, charge us not with a load such as thou didst lay upon those before us. Our Lord, do not thou burden us beyond what we have the strength to bear. And pardon us and forgive us and have mercy upon us. Thou art our Protector, so help us against the people of the unbelievers."

Such a prayer as this is eloquent enough testimony to the

spiritual value of life as seen by Islam. And it may fitly be paralleled by another quotation from the same Sura—II: 186: "And when my servants question thee concerning me, I am near to answer the call of the caller when he calls to me. So let them respond to me and let them believe in me; haply so they will go aright."

But perhaps the most striking testimony of all to the spiritual and selfless meaning of true life in Islam is the constant emphasis in the Qur'an on good works. Consider, for instance, this picture of the true servants of God, those who are realizing the meaning of their life to the fullest. It comes from Sura XXV: 63-76:

> The servants of the All-Merciful are
> those who walk in the earth modestly
> and who, when the ignorant address them,
> say "Peace;"
> who pass the night prostrate to their Lord
> and standing;
> who say, "Our Lord, turn thou from us
> the chastisement of Gehenna;" surely
> its chastisement is torment most terrible;
> evil it is as a lodging-place
> and an abode;
> who, when they expend, are neither prodigal
> nor parsimonious, but between that is
> a just stand;
> who call not upon another god with God,
> nor slay the soul God has forbidden
> except by right, neither fornicate,
> for whosoever does that shall meet
> the price of sin—
> doubled shall be the chastisement for him
> on the Resurrection Day, and he shall dwell
> therein humbled,
> save him who repents, and believes, and
> does righteous work—those God will
> change their evil deeds into good deeds,
> for God is ever All-forgiving,
> All-compassionate;

and whosoever repents and does
righteousness, he truly turns to God
        in repentance.
And those who bear not false witness
and, when they pass by idle talk, pass by
        with dignity;
who, when they are reminded of the signs
of their Lord, fall not down thereat
        deaf and blind;
who say, "Our Lord, give us refreshment of
our wives and seed, and make us a model
        to the godfearing."
Those shall be recompensed with the highest
heaven, for that they endured patiently,
and they shall receive therein a greeting
        and — "Peace!"
Therein they shall dwell forever;
fair it is as a lodging-place
        and an abode.

This is life as the Qur'an sees it being lived to the fullest, the highest and the best—a life of quiet and unassuming virtue and faith. This the life of the individual in submission.

But man is more always than just an individual, important though that may be. He is also a member of a race, a unit in a community, whether religious, social, political or economic; he must associate with other individuals, and thus is raised a whole range of new problems concerning the meaning of life.

We turn now, therefore, to consider the Islamic concept of the meaning of social life, and here the important word is another Arabic term which has become familiar to the West in one particular form. It is the word *khalifa* (plural *khulafa*) which has been westernized as Caliph. Unfortunately the meaning has not accompanied the word into English, since Caliph is taken generally to mean an Eastern potentate or ruler.

In fact the word means a "successor" or "deputy," and the Caliphs of Damascus and Baghdad were so called simply because they were the successors or deputies of the Prophet after his death. In its religious usage it is found nine times in the Qur'an, and each time in the same general context.

In Sura II:30 ff there is an account of creation which reads, in part, as follows. "And when thy Lord said to the angels, 'I am creating a deputy (*khalifa*) on the earth,' they said, 'What? Wilt thou create on it a being who will do corruption there and shed blood, while we proclaim thy praise and call thee holy?' He said, 'Assuredly I know what you know not'."

Here is the thought that man is expressly created as the deputy of God on earth, with power to control and exploit the earth's resources, and to use them as God himself would use them. The fact that the earth was created specifically for man's benefit is, indeed, mentioned in the preceding verse: "It is he who created for you all that is in the earth."

This general sense of the word *khalifa* is found in five of the nine passages where the term is used; it is mankind as a whole which is the deputy of God on earth. But one of these passages leads on to another and slightly different usage of the word.

Sura VI:165 reads thus: "It is he who has appointed you as deputies in the earth, and has raised some of you in rank above others, that he may try you in what he has given you. Surely thy Lord is swift in retribution; and surely he is All-forgiving, All-compassionate."

In this there lies the additional implication that the office of deputy of God may be specialized in a ruler, and this is made explicit in other passages. For instance, in XXXVIII:26 the same word *khalifa* is used of David, the Hebrew king: "Oh David, verily I appoint you a deputy in the earth, so rule the people with justice and do not follow caprice." Power, that is to say, whether it be power over man's natural environment or the power of a ruler over his subjects, is delegated by God to man, and therefore man must use it according to the will of God.

Thus the order of nature is God's provision (*rizk*) for man, and men are permitted, even commanded, to enjoy its fruits within the limits of the Divine revelation. Here again, as we have seen previously, Islam has no conception of the world being an evil place, inimical to the spiritual interests of mankind; nor does it know of the theory of the supposed virtues of asceticism. Sura II: 172 makes this undeniably plain: "Oh believers, eat of the good things wherewith we have provided you, and give thanks to God, if it be he whom you serve."

This is taken to be the lesson of the past spiritual history of humanity, in which the spiritual and physical blessings of God are mentioned in the same breath. Thus in Sura XX: 81, which deals with the desert experiences of Israel: "Oh Children of Israel, we delivered you from your enemy, and we made covenant with you on the right side of the Mount; and we sent down on you manna and quails. Eat of the good things wherewith we have provided you; but exceed not therein, or my anger shall light on you."

The same commandment to enjoy the material blessings of life is laid also on the prophets, as in Sura XXIII: 52, "Oh messengers, eat of the good things and do righteousness; surely I know the things you do."

But the enjoyment of God's provision must always be limited by the principles laid down in his revelation; there are two complementary sides to the proposition—"Eat of the good things" and "do righteousness." Here we meet the familiar idea that Islam is pre-eminently a religion of practicality, one which deals with "doing" as much as with "believing." We have already noticed the summons of the muezzin at the five daily times of prayer: "Come to prayer." But, as Dr. Kenneth Cragg points out in his book, *The Call of the Minaret*, it is not less important that this phrase is followed by a parallel phrase, "Come to goodness (*falah*)."

This is man's function as a deputy of God upon earth. It is so to order his acts and his life as to realize in his human community the ideals which God has made known in his revelation. It is the practice of the principles laid down in the Qur'an for the good government of the ideal Islamic society.

What are these principles? And how and in what fields are they to be applied? These two questions may occupy the remainder of this study.

In the light of the fact that the Qur'an describes man as God's deputy, it is not surprising to find that the underlying principles of Muslim—and universal—society are those of unity and equality. For as all men have one Creator, so they must be on a level footing before him; despite the superficial differences of race and colour, of nationality and class, Islam believes in a fundamental common ground which makes all men one.

The most sweeping declaration of this belief is to be found in the idea, frequently repeated in the Qur'an, that mankind constitutes a single "*umma*," nation, people or community. So in Sura XXIII: 51, "Surely this community of yours is one community, and I am your Lord; so fear me." The Qur'an sees this ultimate unity as the original state of things in the world; so, for example, Sura X: 19 says "Mankind were only one community, then they fell into variance. But for a word that preceded from thy Lord, it had been decided between them already touching their differences." Or, as in Sura XXI: 92, "Surely this community of yours is one community, and I am your Lord; so serve me. But they split up their affair between them; all shall return to us." The important difference between this and the first quotation in this paragraph lies in the closing phrase; the unity which was original will finally be restored, and this is the function of Islam.

This brings us to the second major aspect of unity—that of religion. In order to realize the single *umma* which is the Divine will, Islam is proffered as the universal religion, and Muhammad must proclaim himself as the Apostle of God to all mankind. So we have in Sura VII: 168, "Say, Oh mankind, I am the messenger of God to you all. But it is an invitation, not an imposition."

These last words should make clear the fallacy of the common Western belief that the unity of religion which Islam seeks to realize is one to be enforced. "Islam or the sword" is a phrase which has gained altogether too wide a currency. It is, indeed, satisfactorily refuted by the words of a Western scholar, De Lacy O'Leary (*Islam at the Crossroads,* p. 8): "History makes it clear that the legend of fanatical Muslims sweeping through the world and forcing Islam at the point of the sword upon conquered races is one of the most fantastically absurd myths that historians have ever repeated." Few people, if any, should be unaware that such compulsion is in fact forbidden by the Qur'an itself (Sura II: 256): "There is no compulsion in religion."

Failing this most desirable form of unity, therefore, the Qur'an meets reality by proclaiming the cardinal doctrine of Muslim practice, the brotherhood of all believers. Mankind as a whole may for different reasons resist the call to a universal, common faith; but the ideal of brotherhood can be put into practice among all who follow the teachings of the Prophet. So indeed Muhammad instituted the custom of the brotherhood relation between the Emigrants and the Helpers (the Meccans and the Medinans respectively) at the time of the *Hijra*; and the principle is clearly stated in Sura XLIX: 10: "The believers indeed are brothers; so set things right between your two brothers, and fear God; happily so you will find mercy."

And it is no less than typical of Islam that this equality in religion and in status is extended to all men immediately they join themselves to the Islamic fellowship. There are no second-class citizens in the Muslim community—as is indicated in Sura IX: 11 when, speaking of the heathen, it says, "Yet if they repent, and perform the prayer, and pay the alms, then they are your brothers in religion."

Along with this goes yet another equality, that of legal treatment. It is apparent that all Muslims must stand on a common footing before the Islamic law, but the Qur'an goes further to declare that this impartiality must be extended also to non-Muslims living in a Muslim community. Sura V: 47 ff is of interest here. "So let the people of the Gospel (i.e. the Christians) judge (meaning, apply their law) according to what God has sent down therein. Whosoever judges not according to what God has sent down—they are the ungodly. And we have sent down to thee the Book with the truth, confirming the Book that was before it, and assuring it. So judge between them according to what God has sent down, and do not follow their caprices to forsake the truth that has come to thee. To every one of you we have appointed a right way and an open road."

One final unity may be mentioned here—and one which is attracting ever-increasing interest in the modern world—unity of language. The Qur'an is "an Arabic Qur'an" revealed in that language in the Providence of God, and, at least ideally, Arabic is the universal language of the Islamic community. The Qur'an and the prayers should be known by all Muslims in Arabic; the full acceptance of the language as an international tongue must await the coming of the time when all men are more concerned with a world-wide community than with their private and national preoccupations.

Such are the principles of unity and equality underlying the Muslim idea of human society. In theory, as we have seen, they apply to all mankind; but since, thus far at least, the Islamic invitation to other faiths has been refused, these principles are applied only within the Islamic community itself.

We turn now to the question of how these principles are applied, and in what forms and institutions they manifest themselves. But in so doing we are dealing obviously with a society which is in time, and which therefore is constantly changing. The immediate problem which arises, therefore, is that of the Law (*shari'a*), which is the application of principle to concrete situations. Supposing that in the course of historical development a situation arises which is not covered by the Qur'an, how does Islam bring such a situation into its scheme?

This question is rendered the more acute by the fact that the Qur'an, which is the primary source of legislation, contains in fact very little actual law. The sum total of legislation, indeed, is less than one tenth of the whole, and most of this concerns such matters as marital status. The Qur'an, therefore, in effect states principles, but gives little guidance concerning where and how they are to be applied.

Even the second source of authority, which we have already seen to consist in the Traditions, is not fully satisfactory as an answer to this problem. The on-going course of history soon left behind the period during which genuine Traditions of the Prophet could be accepted, and new situations continued to arise. Hence there developed the Muslim science of jurisprudence (*fiqh*), as a continuing means of applying revealed truth to the needs and queries of a constantly developing society.

The Qur'anic basis for this science is to be found in Sura IV: 58: "Oh ye who believe, obey God and obey his Messenger, and those in authority among you. If you should quarrel in anything, refer it to God and the Messenger, if you believe in God and in the Last Day; that is better and fairer in the issue."

"Those in authority" comprise those who are skilled in expounding and applying the law. Beyond the Qur'an and the Traditions they have established two further sources of authority, *Ijma'*, or consensus, and a final source on which opinion is divided, some accepting *Qiyas* or analogy, and some accepting *Ra'y* or opinion.

"Consensus" as a rule of practice refers to the agreement of those qualified to judge in any age on any matter of faith. It depends for its validity on the idea that the whole community is at least unlikely to go astray in matters of faith. And it depends for its authority on the famous Tradition of the Prophet, "My people will never agree in an error," and on such Qur'anic verses as IV: 115, "Whoso . . . follows a way other than the believers, him we shall turn over to what he has turned to and we shall roast him in Gehenna—an evil home-coming."

Opinion—that is to say, expert private opinion—is less widely and generally accepted as an authoritative source of law. There is a Tradition, however, on which it is based. When Mu'adh was sent by the Prophet to Yemen, the latter asked him, "What will you do when there is a legal case?" He answered, "I shall judge by what I find in the Book of God." The Prophet asked, "And if you do not find it in the Book of God?" "Then I shall judge by the Traditions of the Prophet." Asked Muhammad: "If there is no such thing in the Traditions?" "Then I shall strive with my opinions." Mu'adh related that upon hearing my answer the Prophet tapped on my chest, saying, "Praise be to God who gave guidance to the Messenger for what will satisfy the Messenger of God."

Analogy is easily understood. It consists in expanding the revealed law of the Qur'an by a comparison of any given situation with one which was already envisaged in the Qur'an or the Traditions. For example, the Qur'an prohibits the use of wine; by analogy this prohibition may be legitimately enlarged to include the proscription of distilled spirits, which are not, naturally enough, specifically mentioned in the Qur'an, but which certainly come within the spirit of the prohibition.

The formulation of law deriving from these sources is called *Ijtihad,* which means literally enterprise, initiative, and which conveys the sense of hard and sustained effort. One who is judged capable of *ijtihad* is called a *mujtahid,* and throughout the history of Islam there has been prolonged and sometimes bitter dispute about the powers, the responsibilities and the methods of the *mujtahid,* and indeed about whether or not "the door of *ijtihad*" as the phrase goes, "remains open"—that is to say, whether *ijtihad* is a permanent process, or whether its exercise brings the *shari'a* to a point where no more is needed.

Islamic law, thus derived and applied, is therefore simply the application of the Qur'anic teachings to the practical and concrete situations of life and society by whatever method may be permissible and possible. But one word of warning is in place here. There is a constant danger—for Islam as well as for those who seek to interpret it—that all this mention of "law" should give the impression that Islam is at the mercy of a cold and formal legalism. This is always possible when principles

127

must be codified in legal form; but it is characteristically foreseen and forbidden in the Qur'an itself.

In connection with oaths, for instance, Sura II: 225 has this to say: "God will not take you to task for a slip in your oath; but he will take you to task for what your hearts have earned; and God is All-forgiving, All-compassionate." Or, more generally, Sura XXXIII: 5 runs thus: "There is no fault in you if you make mistakes, but only in what your hearts premeditate. God is All-forgiving, All-compassionate."

And the same warning is specifically issued in regard to the danger of that empty and formal religious legalism which consists in fulfilling the "letter of the law" while ignoring the spirit. Sura XXII: 37 reads, in connection with sacrifice, "And the beasts of sacrifice we have appointed them for you as among God's waymarks; therein is good for you. So mention God's name over them, standing in your ranks; then, when their flanks collapse, eat of them, and feed the beggar and the suppliant. So we have subjected them to you; haply you will be thankful. The flesh of them shall not reach God, neither their blood; but godliness from you shall reach him."

It is the spirit, rather than the precise letter, which Islamic law seeks to apply to society as a means of expressing the full religious meaning of human life. And in conclusion we may now turn to see how these revealed principles of justice, unity and equality, which express man's function as God's deputy, are put into effect in the different aspects of the life of the Islamic community.

In religion the Islamic community pays obvious homage to the idea of equality among men as God's deputies. No individual can stand in any closer or more intimate relation to God than any other; therefore Islam has no priesthood nor any sacramental system, no clergy nor church organization. Any Muslim may serve as *Imam* or leader of public worship. The ranks of the faithful in the mosque (*masjid,* literally a place of prostration), facing the *qibla,* the direction of Mecca, and following the *Imam* through the pattern of the prayers, are the most

128

vivid testimony to the unity and equality which pervade Muslim worship.

The Arabic name for the prayers, *salat,* which really means supplication with adoration, is a constant affirmation of the dependence of man upon God, a reliance which is thus brought to the Muslim's mind five times a day. For at dawn, at midday, in late afternoon, at sunset and again before retiring for the night the Muslim is called to pray in recognition of the God who is ever in the midst of human life. Nor need he go to a mosque for the purpose of worship. Every Muslim's prayer-mat is his private mosque, and he may say his prayers wherever he happens to be at the prescribed time.

This democratic spirit in religion, which, however, is never permitted to degenerate into anarchy, is still further illustrated in another of the five "pillars" of the faith—the *Hajj* or Pilgrimage to Mecca. Just as the *mihrab* or niche in the mosque serves to orient the worshippers towards Mecca in spirit, so the Qur'an lays on loyal believers the duty of performing the *Hajj* at least once in a lifetime. Sura III: 92 expresses it thus: "It is the duty of all men towards God to come to the House a pilgrim, if he is able to make his way there."

In this observance the universal equality of Muslims is made manifest. From all corners of the Islamic world men meet as brothers within the faith, without distinction of colour, race or social standing. All wear the same pilgrim garments, and all perform the same ceremonies. And the spirit of the occasion is best illustrated by the pilgrim cry of *Labbaika,* often repeated, which Dr. Cragg maintains should be translated as "Doubly at thy service, O God." The Pilgrimage is the living embodiment of the Muslim's belief that his life finds meaning only when it is spent in service as God's deputy, and in the context of the great world-wide unity which is the Islamic ideal.

When we turn to political theory in Islam, we find another clear illustration of the idea of man as God's deputy. The organization of a state rests on authority, claimed and accepted by rulers and people respectively. But all authority belongs ultimately to God alone, and therefore the sovereignty exercised by men is delegated by God. When this is viewed in the Qur'anic light of the principle of the equality of all believers, it means inevitably that authority belongs to the members of the religious community. Church and State, in other and more familiar terms, are one and the same.

This is the teaching of the Qur'an, which, when it speaks of public affairs, uses a grammatical construction in the second person plural, indicating that the community as a company of believers is being addressed. Authority, in other words, resides in the *Umma* or community, which has the power of *Shura* or consultation.

This is maintained by the Qur'am, which says (Sura LII: 159), "Oh Muhammad, consult with them (the Believers) in public affairs;" or, in direct reference to the religious community, (XL: 38), "Their business is done by consultation among them." Thus, at least in theory, the Caliph, normally regarded as the head of the Muslim state, is in reality, as his name implies, no more than the successor or deputy of the Prophet, and the authority of the State is vested, as in the primitive Islamic community, in him together with the representatives of the people, who are known in Islam as the "men who tie and untie."

But the responsibility for the proper administration of the State lies with the religious community. This is a clear Qur'anic prescription for the administering of justice, that most characteristic office of the public authority. Justice is one of the attributes of God, and man, as His deputy must be equally observant of the paramount claims of justice. Two quotations from Suras IV and V make this unmistakably clear; first, from Sura V: 9: "Oh believers, be you securers of justice, witnesses for God. Let not detestation for a people move you not to be equitable; be equitable, that is nearer to God-fearing. And fear God; surely God is aware of the things you do." This bluntly forbids prejudice of any kind, but particularly racial prejudice and verse 135 of Sura IV goes even further, to prohibit preju dice on family or social grounds. "Oh believers, be you securers of justice, witnesses for God, even though it be against yourself or your parents and kinsmen, whether the man be rich or poor; God stands closest to either. Then follow not caprice, so as to swerve; for if you twist or turn, God is aware of the things you do."

Another primary responsibility of the State, which may be taken here as an example, is the power of peace and war, that momentous decision which must profoundly affect the lives and fortunes of all citizens. We have already noticed the fallacy of the common belief that Islam is propagated as a matter of policy by war. But there is an Islamic institution known as *Jihad,* generally rendered as "holy war", but meaning literally striving or effort.

Jihad therefore does not necessarily mean war in the accepted sense of the term. The Muslim jurists, in fact, distinguish four different forms of *Jihad*: by the heart, by the tongue, by the hands, and by the sword—of which only the last is religious "war" in the full sense of the term, which has as its objective the spread of the true faith among idolaters, and which demands the sacrifice of 'wealth and life" by the believer (Sura LXI: 11).

Outside of this purpose Islam forbids altogether the waging of aggressive war, and countenances fighting only in self-defence. So Sura II: 186: "And fight in the way of God with those who fight with you, but aggress not; God loves not the aggressor."

Similarly the sometimes desperate situation of the primitive Muslim community is reflected in such passages of the Qur'an as comment on the reason for such defensive war—namely, that, failing it, the community might well have perished. Such a passage is Sura XXII: 38-41: "Assuredly God will defend those who believe; surely God loves not any ungrateful traitor. Leave is given to those who fight because they were wronged—surely God is able to help them—who were expelled from their habitations without right, except that they say 'Our Lord is

131

God.' Had God not driven back the people, some by means of others, there had been destroyed cloisters and churches, oratories and mosques, wherein God's name is much mentioned. Assuredly God will help him who helps him—surely God is All-strong, All-mighty—who, if we establish them in the land, perform the prayer, and pay the alms, and bid to honour and forbid dishonour; and unto God belongs the issue of affairs."

This speaks for itself as a belief in the sole justification for war as being the maintenance and the preservation of the social and religious values for which Islam stands. Further, this emphasis on the permissibility of war only as a last resort for self-preservation receives further emphasis from the teaching that peace is always better than war and is therefore always to be preferred. So Sura VIII: 61, "And if they (the unbelievers) incline to peace, do thou incline to it, and put thy trust on God. He is the All-hearing, the All-knowing."

But the preceding verse well expresses in Arabic the truth of the old Latin saying, *Si pacem vis, bellum para*: "Make ready for them whatever force and strings of horses you can, to terrify thereby the enemy of God, and your enemy, and others besides them that you know not; God knows them. And whatsoever you expend in the way of God (i.e. religious war) shall be repaid you in full; you will not be wronged."

These are the principles of war which are binding on the State. Man, as God's deputy, must abhor war as a waste of the Divine endowment; but if pacifism means the danger of the extinction of the faith, then war becomes allowable. But at all times it is the membership of the community, and not the man at the head of it, which has the power of decision.

It is not really possible to separate the thought of society in Islam from the thought of the state or the faith. All are inter-related, since all are based on the one source, the Qur'an. Yet we may turn to the form assumed by the Islamic society to see further evidence of what we have observed already— man's responsibility as a deputy of God.

The most typical Islamic institution here is that of *Zakat,*

132

the obligatory almsgiving which is commanded in the Qur'an, and which forms another of the "five pillars" of the faith. The importance of the other four, Profession of faith, Prayer, Fasting and Pilgrimage, we have already noticed.

Zakat expresses the Islamic belief that man's stewardship of the world's resources is not for himself alone, but in the interests of society, and particularly in the care for the less fortunate members of the community. Two types of almsgiving are commanded in the Qur'an; one, the *Sadaqat,* is purely voluntary and individual; the other is *Zakat,* which is statutory and consists in the compulsory contribution of a certain fixed proportion of income annually into a communal fund for disbursement in certain specified directions.

This compulsory giving of alms has frequent and strong Qur'anic authority, being frequently associated with Prayer as the distinguishing mark of the Muslim. One passage especially well describes the good life in Islam—Sura II: 177: "It is not piety, that you turn your faces to the East and to the West. True piety is this: to believe in God and the Last Day, the angels, the Book, and the Prophets, to give of one's substance, however cherished, to kinsmen and orphans, the needy, the traveller, beggars, and to ransom the slave, to perform the prayer, to pay the alms."

This represents the ideal of Islamic social life as neither capitalism nor socialism. Possessions on the one hand are regarded not as the inalienable right of the possessor, but as an endowment to be employed in the public good as well as in private enjoyment. On the other hand, responsibility for the welfare of society is not the care of the impersonal state, but of the individual Muslim.

Two other aspects of Islamic social life, which have often been misrepresented, may engage our attention here: the position of women, and the institution of slavery.

It is completely untrue to maintain that Islam "degraded" womankind. On the contrary, Islam gave to woman as a sex for the first time a position which they had hitherto been denied.

From the beginning the Prophet set his face resolutely against the familiar pre-Islamic custom of exposing female infants to die. To pagan Arabia the birth of a son was an inestimable blessing in a family—an occasion, like the appearance of a poet in the tribe, for rejoicing; but the birth of a daughter was, in blunt terms, only another mouth to feed. Hence the custom of leaving female children to die, or of burying them alive Thus Sura XVII: 33, "And slay not your children for fear of poverty; We will provide for you and them; surely the slaying of them is a grievous sin." Or again in Sura LXXXI: 9 f. "When the buried infant shall be asked for what sin she was slain . . . then shall a soul know what it has produced."

In point of religious duties and social privileges the Qur'an makes no distinction between men and women. So Sura IX 72, "And the believers, the men and the women, are friend one of another; they bid to honour, and they forbid dishonour they perform the prayer and pay the alms, and they obey God and his Messenger. These—upon them God will have mercy God is All-mighty, All-wise. God has promised the believers men and women, gardens underneath which rivers flow, foreve therein to dwell."

Or again, from Sura IV, the title of which is "The Sura o Women," comes this precise definition of the legal inheritanc rights of women and men alike: "To the men a share of what parents and kinsmen leave, and to the women a share of what parents and kinsmen leave, whether it be little or much, a shar apportioned."

The Qur'an does not, however, fall into the trap of unrealit by any sweeping assertion of the complete equality of th sexes. Men and women are created differently, and have dif ferent responsibilities. "Women have such honourable right as obligations, but their men have a degree above them; God i All-mighty, All-wise" (Sura II: 228). Or, "Men are th managers of the affairs of women, for that God has preferre in bounty one of them over another, and for that they hav expended of their property" (Sura IV: 33).

But the most frequently misunderstood Islamic social institution is polygamy. Islam did not originate polygamy; it limited it as a practice to the possession of four wives, and it limited it even further by the provision that there must be no discrimination; all wives must be treated with scrupulous fairness, and unless this is possible, financially and otherwise, multiplicity of wives is forbidden. There may be many reasons for polygamy as a social ordinance—excessive virility, the desire to discourage extra-marital relationships, the excess of women in a population suffering from wars, and so on; but the keynote of the Qur'an's treatment of the subject is to be found in Sura IV: 23, "Consort with them honourably."

Islam therefore seeks to check the licence which is all too often found in all societies between the sexes. It is often pointed out that Muhammad himself, the model of Islamic life, had several wives; but while his first wife Khadija lived, she was the only one, and their mutual affection never seems to have wavered.

None the less the husband is always regarded as the head of the household, and his authority may be exercised in various ways, the most desirable of which is the virtue called in Arabic *ḥilm,* generally translated as "clemency", but really indicating more the ability to exert one's authority without recourse to violent methods of persuasion. For the same reason divorce in Islam is placed normally in the hands of the man as dominant partner in the marriage, and because the maintenance of the family is primarily his responsibility. But in order to avoid the complete subjugation of women, the wife is entitled to her right to seek divorce before a judge.

A final example of social responsibility in Islam may be drawn from slavery. This universal custom at the time of the appearance of Islam arose generally out of conquest in war. It was therefore accepted as the prevailing practice, and the really significant thing is that Islam saw it as so much of a moral problem as to legislate for its mitigation as far as possible.

Muhammad, for instance, recommended the freeing of all such slaves as requested manumission, and himself set the example by liberating all his own slaves before his death. Little else, indeed, could be expected of a religion which proclaimed so fervently the fundamental equality of all men, and the impetus towards the abolition of slavery is to be seen in several facts.

The slave under Islam was able to work on his own account, and to save his earnings towards the payment of his own ransom. A female slave who bore a child to her master was freed immediately on the death of her master, while the child was born free. The act of freeing slaves was made the full atonement for certain sins. As we have seen, the ransoming of slaves was one of the accepted ways in which the *Zakat* monies were disbursed, and in addition rich Muslims were encouraged to free their slaves as a mark of piety.

Nothing tests a society like its use of wealth, and we may close this brief consideration of the meaning of life in the Islamic society by looking at its economic theory. We have already seen the doctrine of the social responsibility of wealth in connection with *Zakat,* but there is much more than this in the teaching of the Qur'an.

Islam clearly ratifies the right of individual possession by legal means of acquisition. It has no affinity with communist or socialist ideas of state control or state possession. Further it safeguards that right of private possession by stringent laws against theft and plunder. The punishment for theft is stated in Sura V: 42, "And the thief, male and female: cut off the hands of both, as a recompense for what they have earned and as a punishment exemplary from God." The enjoyment of what he has legally earned is one of the rights of man as the deputy of God, who gives all things to man.

But at the same time the Qur'an is well aware of the danger of riches. At best they are a test of the character of their owner, with the possibility of bringing out either good or evil which may be latent in him. "You will be tested in your wealth

136

and in your own selves" (Sura III: 186); and the basic Islamic doctrine of worldly goods is put into the mouth of Solomon in Sura XXVII: 40, when, having received the throne of the Queen of Sheba, he said, "This is of my Lord's bounty that he may try me, whether I am thankful or ungrateful." In any case wealth is regarded as something secondary to the more important spiritual values—"Wealth and sons are the adornment of life in this world. But the abiding things, the deeds of righteousness, are better with God in reward and better in hope."

This note of warning against the perils of riches is struck frequently in the Qur'an, on the well-founded grounds that possessions breed a false sense of security and a blindness to spiritual values, in which the true function of material things is forgotten. "Surely man waxes insolent when he finds himself rich. Surely unto the Lord is the returning" (Sura XCVI: 6-8). "Woe unto every backbiter, slanderer, who has gathered riches and counted them over, thinking his riches have made him immortal" (Sura CIV: 1-3).

Allied to this is the danger of an unbridled exercise of the acquisitive spirit. Wealth breeds the hunger for more wealth. Miserliness is one of the most frequently condemned sins in the Qur'an, and it is but the more despicable when it is placed in the context of the belief that all things are of the Divine bounty. Sura III: 180 puts this very clearly: "But as for those who are niggardly with the bounty God has given them, let them not suppose it is better for them; nay, it is worse for them. That with which they were niggardly they shall have hung about their necks on the Resurrection Day." It is the sharp contrast here between the words 'niggardly" and "bounty" which brings out the full lesson. What God has freely given, that man must not hoard.

On the other hand, possibly as a reaction against the pre-Islamic custom of open-handed prodigality, practised sometimes to the point of beggaring its proponents, Islam deprecates unwise expenditure when it is merely a self-conscious expression of lavishness. The "happy mean" is advocated in Sura XXV 67, which describes good Muslims as those "Who when they expend are neither prodigal nor parsimonious, but between that is a just stand."

We have already noticed the obligation to society in the Zakat and in the voluntary *Sadaqat*. This is the true stewardship, which man, as deputy of God on earth, must exercise of the things with which he is endowed. Wealth, in other words, is something given by God, and therefore something to be used in service to God. Sura IV : 95 puts it succinctly: "Such believers as sit at home—unless they have an injury—are not the equals of those who struggle in the Way of God with their possessions and with their selves. God has preferred in rank those who struggle with their possessions and with their selves over the ones who sit at home. Yet to each God has promised reward most fair."

The meaning of life can be understood only in the context of the Giver of life and his purposes for his creation. Islam is a religion, and consequently its interpretation of life is basically theological. A Book which is the supreme rule for faith and life, as it is the unquestioned self-revelation of God, given through Muhammad, His Prophet—this is the Islamic Scripture. An inner life of the spirit which is founded on the principle that man's supreme good is to submit to God as he has made himself known in history—this is the ideal for the Muslim individual. A society, which is still limited by the reluctance of others to yield to its authority, but which consists in moderation, regard for the rights of others, in the unity and the equality of all men before their Creator, and which is inspired by the ultimate hope that eventually its virtues and values may become universal—this is the society of Islam. The spirit of the whole may best be expressed in the opening verse of the first Sura of the Qur'an, the *Fatiha: Al-hamdu lillah, rabb al-'alamain*—Praise belongs to God, the Lord of both the worlds.

C. DOUGLAS JAY

VII. FROM ENCOUNTER TO COMMUNITY

The preceding chapters are offered as instruments of that open encounter called for in Dr. Taylor's introduction. Their authors have avoided the temptation to write defensively, and have undertaken to expound their distinctive positions with the honesty and permissiveness that are requisite in such a conversation. One of the hopeful aspects of the present world situation is that this kind of free encounter is possible and indeed finds encouragement from within most religious traditions as well as within academic circles. When differences are out in the open, there is more hope of true understanding of men of other faiths and less danger of the distortions that are inevitable when we are invited to meet straw men. When men are disposed to recognize their differences, the genuine Christian may enter into dialogue with the genuine Jew, the true Hindu, the authentic Muslims and the real Buddhist.

Opportunities to study non-Christian religions have increasingly been available during the last century through data gathered in the fields of literature, philology, philosophy and anthropology. But serious encounter and conversation with representatives of other faiths have been inhibited by the tendency on the part of Westerners to alternate between two extreme types of response. The one extreme reflects the scepticism inherited from the Age of Enlightenment, which tended to regard the various religions as essentially identical in content and motivation.[1] The other extreme which characterized the response of conservative Christians was represented by the view that there was little that was theologically significant in Islam,

[1] *Vide* Joachim Wach, *The Journal of Religion*, vol. xxvii, no. 3, July 1947, p. 159.

the religions of India and the Far East, and therefore they could be ignored without serious loss to the cause of truth.

While the West in general and the Christian community in particular are still by no means free from these attitudes, the urgent need of establishing a foundation for world community has helped to convince many that neither contempt for the faiths of other men nor a blurring of real differences between them will meet the crisis confronting men in the second half of the twentieth century. By world community we do not mean an ordered world society—this may never become a reality —but a significant degree of world-wide consciousness of human solidarity and of what is shared in common, together with respect for real differences.

One obvious limitation of the present inquiry is that the representatives of the various faiths have not had any sort of direct encounter with each other in the presentation of their papers. What is offered here is thus not an example of encounter or conversation but data which may assist the reader to participate in such an encounter with greater understanding. Admittedly, understanding alone is not enough; it is no substitute for reconciliation, and this has been the weakness of proposals for the unification of world cultures on a purely intellectual basis, such as those advanced by F. S. C. Northrop in *The Meeting of East and West*. Nevertheless, there is no substitute for understanding and the present theme is of peculiar importance. The contemporary crisis may serve to remind us that the classic affirmations of the world's great religions have generally been formulated under the shadow of adversity; crisis motivates reflection on the nature of man, the meaning of his life and the shape of his destiny. Edward J. Jurji has pointed out that "the humanism of Confucius, the meditation of India, the resignation of Islam and the rationalism of so much in modern Judaism, stemmed from the quest for a deeper and more valid understanding of man and his destiny."[2] It is all

---

[2]E. J. Jurji, *The Christian Interpretation of Religion*, (New York: Macmillan, 1952), p. 291.

the more remarkable that although much has been written in the general area of the comparative study of religion, little attempt has been made to compare what the world religions have to say on so central a theme. If Gerald Cooke is right in affirming that "the question of the meaning of existing as a human being is recognized today more widely than ever as a fundamentally religious and theological question,"[3] the attempt to provide representative answers to the question is more than justified at a time when all the large issues of life must be faced in a context that is world-wide.

The crucial problem posed by the foregoing chapters for mid-twentieth-century man is surely that of how, given a diversity of answers to so relevant a question, community can be established on a world scale. Prophetic voices in many quarters—science, politics and religion among them—warn us repeatedly that human development has reached the point where some kind of world order must be constructed or we perish. On the other hand, men of the stature of Reinhold Niebuhr have warned that the possibility of establishing an effective world order remains slender, at least for decades to come.[4] Most agree however, that it is a goal toward which we must strive, and one condition of its achievement may be an effective sense of world community. The technological and economic and political aspects of "one world" are under active consideration by able men and influential groups; but the ideological, moral and spiritual aspects of human cohesion have received less attention, though in the last analysis they may prove more crucial. If humanity is to progress toward global integration in any significant form, the religious dimension cannot be ignored. Cooperation among men of diverse religions is imperative for even the minimum degree of worldmindedness necessary for survival.

[3] In *As Christians Face Rival Religions*, (New York: Association Press, 1962), p. 177.
[4] In *The Structure of Nations and Empires*, (New York: Scribners, 1959), pp. 29, 33.

If this is true, it will not be enough for men to encounter each other; encounter cannot be accepted as an end in itself but must be accepted as an instrument of establishing community on a broader and deeper scale than heretofore.

Is there any significant measure of consensus about the need for community in the religious traditions here examined? Is a concern for community a significant part of each tradition's answer to the question of the meaning of life? We shall review the preceding chapters with these questions in mind.

HINDUISM

In Professor Nagaraja Rao's exposition of the Hindu view of the meaning of life there is little explicit reference to community whether on a local or world scale. Moreover, the application of the concept of Maya to life in the world and the identification of man with the non-dual Spirit which constitutes ultimate reality appear to be so seriously at odds with the Hebrew-Christian conceptions of God, man and the world that one is disposed to give up any attempt to find common ground with respect to so this-worldly a concern as world community. Although Hinduism is all-embracing in that all descriptions of the Absolute are said to be equally true—as the *Rgveda* puts it, "Reality is one and wise men call it by various names and approach it by many paths"[5]—yet the differences between Hinduism and the Hebrew-Christian approach are significant and are not minimized. Professor Rao distinguishes between "ordinary theism" which believes in both God and the world and Sankara's position which affirms belief only in God, and is thus "super-theism."[6] "Outside the Spirit everything is unreal," according to Sankara.[7] Moreover, "there is no organic

[5] *Supra*, p. 36.
[6] Rao quotes with approval S. Chatterjee and D. M. Dutta on this point.
[7] *Supra*, p. 28.

142

connection between the Absolute Spirit and the world of appearance," and "the Spirit is in no way affected by the blemishes and the taints present in empirical existence."[8] It is in the light of this concept of ultimate reality that one must understand the concept of maya as applied to the created order, the world of appearance. Professor Rao is careful to reject the criticism that for Sankara, the world is regarded as illusory. This is an oversimplification amounting to a distortion. For according to Sankara, the world has objective, empirical reality in a way that a dream does not; but only the Absolute is ultimately real.

The world is thus not unreal, though it exists only on a secondary level of reality; and on this level we have "plurality of souls." This is the sense in which the world is regarded as illusion, according to the theory of maya; for the eternal Spirit which is One appears as many, in the empirical order. Moreover, the plurality of souls are competing, conflicting centres of life. It is at this point that we might have expected a concern for community to emerge, as a solution to the problem of conflict. But from the standpoint of Advaita-Vedanta, the solution is rather to transcend the world of maya, to "break this pluralist illusion and realize the unitive experience."[9] Mystic union is the high destiny of man. But this in turn has implications for empirical life, for it provides a basis for inspiring selflessness in man. Professor Rao goes so far as to quote with approval a claim that the basis for fulfilling the biblical injunction to love your neighbour as yourself lies not in the Bible but in Sankara's formula "That Thou Art." "You shall love your neighbour as yourself because you are in essence non-different from your neighbour."[10] The "unitive" or "spiritual" experience through which man realizes unity with the divine also provides the basis for realizing universal human unity.[11]

---

[8]*Loc. cit.*
[9]*Supra,* p. 29.
[10]*Supra,* p. 30.
[11]*Loc. cit.*

Christians will take issue with the claim that this "highest law of morality" finds a more adequate basis in Advaitan philosophy than in the Gospel, but the significant thing for our immediate purposes is that this law is recognized as the summit of morality, and a basis sought for it.

It is apparent then that the Advaitan doctrine which regards Supreme Reality as eternally distinct from the empirical world and which has encouraged Hinduism's world-negating tendencies, may also lead to world-affirmation. The conviction that Brahman is the source and undergirding power of all that is, yields the further conviction of the sanctity of all living beings. While individuality is something to be transcended (in spiritual union) personality is affirmed.[12] Spiritual realization, the goal of human life, may be a present reality as well as an eschatological hope, and is said to be in full accord with Schweitzer's "reverence for life." It is fair to add that these world-affirming tendencies of Hinduism are much older than Sankara. The Code of Manu which predates Sankara by many centuries expressed a concern to balance world-denying tendencies with this-worldly emphasis, and states that withdrawal from life in society should be reserved for one's later years. The ideal Hindu life of the Four Ashramas should begin with moral training as well as education in ascetic disciplines; the second stage is to be one of *full participation in social responsibilities,* and only in the third and fourth call for withdrawal from life in society and the world.

It is apparent therefore that in spite of a valuation of history and the world that differs substantially from the Hebrew-Christian, there is nevertheless a basis in Hinduism for not only encountering the neighbour but affirming his worth and establishing community with him.[13] If it be objected that there is a contradiction between the world-denying and the world-affirm-

---

[12]See below pp. 146-7 for a discussion of this in relation to Buddhism.

[13]F. H. Ross describes the "enlightened" person as one of "sensitized spirit and conscience" who "works with a new sense of the interconnectedness of all society." *Vide The Meaning of Life in Hinduism and Buddhism.* (London: Routledge and Kegan Paul Ltd., 1952), p. 71.

ing tendencies of Hinduism, it may be replied that such a contradiction characterizes most religions that are living realities, that Hindus have managed to live with such inconsistencies for at least twenty-five centuries, and that the very diversity of Hinduism strengthens its claim to be the truly universal faith in offering something for a variety of temperaments.

BUDDHISM

In the exposition of the Buddhist conception of the meaning of life, as with the Hindu, little is said directly about concern for community, though certain implications are relevant. The supreme goal of life is an escape from suffering, and it is evident that a good deal of suffering originates in community relationships. The inter-relationship of all things and events which the author stresses must include events of our common life, and these largely determine our present and future happiness. The meaning of life is "to realize that it is only possible for one to live in this present world through innumerable direct and indirect causes which come from all others, and the purpose of life is to live everyday . . . in the consciousness of how I am happy to be born a human being and that every deed will be the indirect cause for others in the future."[14] The meaning and purpose of life are further defined in terms of living in a state of real happiness through realizing that the world is impermanent and that one should be grateful to all other existences. Thus, "to live in this present society as a human being itself is the meaning of life," to which is subsequently added "seeing all existences and phenomena as they are."[15] This presumably includes taking serious account of social relationships.

Further, we note that the Eightfold Right Path which is designed to deliver man from suffering includes the "Right Way

---

[14] *Supra,* p. 54.
[15] *Loc. cit.*

145

of Life *in Society.*" Little indication is given, however, of a concern for society itself; the emphasis seems to be on how one may avoid suffering in social relationships, though the emphasis on "Right Words (which are true)" and "Right Conduct" would undoubtedly contribute to the strengthening of the fabric of society. Buddhism is affirmed to be a religion of selflessness, but this turns out to be not the concern for the neighbour with which we are familiar in the Christian ethic so much as a denial that the self has any permanent existence. It is evident that in Buddhism as in Hinduism there is a very different evaluation of individuality from that to which Western man is accustomed. Professor Keijji Nishitani[16] criticizes the preoccupation of Westerners with civil rights on the ground that it represents too individualistic an approach to the problems of society. While we may not agree with the philosophic presuppositions of the criticism, we may recognize the validity of the protest that an individualistic approach even to human rights can vitiate a real sense of community.

Although Dr. Hanayama has not stressed the Buddhist concept of love (*maitrî*), it is instructive at this point to compare it with the Christian concept of love as *agape*. The apparent contrast which is often drawn between the Christian love of neighbour in terms of outgoing sacrificial concern and Buddhist statements about rejecting all personal attachments and relationships—love as well as hate—is based on a gross over-simplification. Buddhism rejects love in the sense of liking, desire or craving, but Northern or Mahayana Buddhism stresses the Buddha's example of unbounded compassion for all living beings. It has been suggested that such love (*maitrî*) is the purest form of charity since it extends beyond men to all creatures, even to vegetation.

A real difference becomes apparent however between the Christian and Buddhist conception of "neighbour." Christian

---

[16]A leading Buddhist philosopher (on the faculty of Kyoto University) in an interview with the present writer in 1963.

love is directed toward the neighbour as a concrete individual, though an individual-in-community. Buddhism regards the neighbour's individuality as ultimately unreal and of no abiding significance. Both Christian *agape* and Buddhist *maitrî* consist in loving one's neighbour as oneself. But whereas the former is a relationship between two equally real individualities, both created in the image of God, the latter occurs between two equally "suffering, impermanent and unsubstantial aggregates," in the classic phrase. As Henri de Lubas says, "Since it is not taken seriously [the individuality of our fellow man] can not be the object of a serious love."[17] A Buddhist must love the individuality of his neighbour as little as his own, for only the universal "self" (*âtmâ*) is real, and this is why *maitrî* can and should be extended equally to man, animals and plants. *Maitrî* is compassion, an attitude of identification with all living, suffering beings.

Jacques-Albert Cuttat has stressed the radical breach between *agape* and *maitrî* at this point.[18] Christian love is extended to the neighbour as a fellow creature and thus must be concentrated on man; it is thus different from and more than Buddhist compassion, which "loses in intensity what it gains in breadth."[19] Christian love embraces compassion for all creatures, but instead of reducing *agape* to compassion, the latter is subordinated to the former. Christian compassion is centred in love of man because man is the epitome of the entire creation and is thus responsible for the destiny of all living creatures.[20]

A related difference noted by Cuttat is that *agape* is an end in itself because its object (the human person) is the image and likeness of a God who is love itself. *Maitrî* on the other hand

[17] *Aspects du Bouddhisme*, p. 36.

[18] *The Encounter of Religions* (New York: Desclee Company, Tournai, Paris, Rome, 1960), pp. 59 ff.

[19] *Loc. cit.*

[20] *Ibid*, notes on pp. 65-6.

is a means subordinate to an end other than love, namely *nirvâna*. This final state is regarded as being beyond love since it implies that there is no longer any consciousness of the individuality of either oneself or the neighbour. Buddhist love becomes self love by turning into love of the universal Self (*âtmâ*). Cuttat observes, "Far from growing outward the neighbour, *maitrî* is neutralized in him; 'He who has a hundred kinds of love has a hundred kinds of suffering . . . he who has no love has no suffering,' preached the Buddha. He held that solidarity with the neighbour's suffering consists essentially in 'interchanging one's own ego with that of others'; this solidarity is an ideal 'raft' on which to cross the bitter stream of existence, but (he added) one does not carry a raft on one's shoulders once the other bank is reached."[21]

While this position can be well documented, Cuttat has not done full justice to the concept of love that provides one of the two great Buddhist communities, the Mahayana, with the substance of their reigning ideal, the Bodhisattva. The latter is one who is committed to the path of the Buddha, the way to Buddhahood or enlightenment. In pursuing this path the ideal Mahayana Buddhist follows the great pathfinder, the Buddha himself, in postponing indefinitely entry into the blessed state of *nirvâna* with its final release from suffering, in order to pursue a compassionate ministry to all living (and therefore suffering) beings.

In view of this, it would appear that the differences between the Christian and Buddhist interpretations of love are not in all respects irreconcilable. The Buddha's antipathy toward love has to do with an attitude of self-concern that makes inordinate demands upon life, craving for what life is unable to give. The Christian can share something of this concern, and may recognize here not only the possibility of a creative encounter with the Buddhist but the possibility of a shared concern for community.

[21]*Ibid*, p. 61.

It is apparent from Professor Fackenheim's account that for Judaism, the meaning of human life is defined in terms of "the meeting between the divine and the human." The significance of this meeting is expressed, in part at least, in the *mutuality* of the Divine-human relationship. God and man are not equal partners, it is clear; God initiates the relationship, and bases it on a covenant to which he remains faithful in spite of man's unfaithfulness. Thus the meaning of life for Judaism is centred in community, as founded on the divine covenant which defines the obligations of man-in-community. Nor is this meaning valid only for a limited community, a select group—the Biblical God is the God of all nations. But as God meets man, he meets not an abstraction but a unique individual or a unique group. As Professor Fackenheim puts it, "The commandment to become a holy people unto God (Exod. 16: 6) constitutes Israel as a unique people . . . [and] the rabbis teach that God has made each man unique and speaks to him in his uniqueness."[22]

To be singled out by God is a central source of the meaning of life, we are told; but "the covenant between God and man has from the outset a scope which transcends Israel; and it is only a question of time until this scope encompasses the whole human race."[23]

There is therefore in Judaism a basis for community which embraces both particularism and universalism. Professor Fackenheim goes on to show how these concepts, which are so often regarded as mutually exclusive alternatives by modern man, are united in the Jewish understanding of history. In Judaism history is taken with the utmost seriousness as each event is seen as unique; but each unique event is seen in terms of a universal whole as God is seen to give direction to history. God is "lord of *all* history, encompassing not only the whole past but the whole future as well, including its Messianic consum-

[22] *Supra*, p. 64.
[23] *Supra*, p. 64.

mation."[24] The Hebrew prophets exhibit clearly just how the particular and the universal are combined: they do not proclaim a universally applicable general principle, but they are called by God, the lord of all history, to be men of their time and to speak, in the name of the divine, to the present needs of men. But "though a man of his time, the prophet is not for his time alone. His moment is an epoch-making moment significant for all history."[25] This singling out is not, however, as it is so often misunderstood to be, an act of favouritism on the part of God; the prophet may be singled out for "inescapable agony" and the people whom he addresses may also be called to share his suffering. This is particularity, but not the sort of exclusive particularity popularly attributed to Judaism, and it is one moreover which includes a fundamental concern for the community of mankind.

The Jewish concept of community is also one which rejects the "disjunction of "collectivism' and 'individualism'."[26] The individual is never reduced to his communal or historical role. The Jewish liturgy dramatizes the truth that the individual stands before God in radical solitariness, while in the midst of the congregation. Both individual and community are affirmed to be chosen by God, and sustained by him in spite of man's individual and corporate failures. But to be chosen by God is to be an instrument of a purpose that is world-wide in scope, and which embraces the future as well as present and past. It is clear however, that the eschatological expectation of the consummation of history does not render this world meaningless. According to Professor Fackenheim, "Redemption must consummate both the history in which men work and wait, and the lives of the individuals who work and wait in it."[27] History is to be taken with utter seriousness by man because God has taken it so seriously as to enter it and become involved in it;

[24] *Loc. cit.*
[25] *Supra,* p. 65.
[26] *Supra,* p. 72.
[27] *Supra,* p. 78.

thus the attempt to establish a satisfactory basis for human community within history becomes an enterprise of the greatest importance.

While the primary locus of meaning for Christianity is the "new covenant," all that has been said above concerning the importance of history and human community in this world in terms of the "old" or "first" covenant is affirmed by Christians as central in their heritage. Although Christians centre the meaning of human life in God's entry into history in Jesus Christ rather than in terms of the Commandment, the latter is not negated but regarded as fulfilled in Jesus Christ. Without minimizing their differences, Christians and Jews ought to find themselves in fundamental accord as to the basis of human community.

CHRISTIANITY

Christianity affirms with Judaism that the meaning of human life is derived from God's meeting with man, and shares the concern of both Judaism and Islam to emphasize God's sovereignty. "Man's chief end is to glorify God and enjoy him forever," from this perspective. But the nature of God in terms of *agape* love is stressed, so that man's response is defined in terms of answering love rather than submission as in Islam. As Professor Chalmers puts it, "The Christian maintains that it is love that gives life its true purpose and worth. But we can only discern this worth as we believe that love reigns supreme on the throne of the universe, that God's name and nature is love."[28] For the Christian this is revealed decisively in Jesus Christ who is "love incarnate." The meaning of life then is revealed in Jesus Christ, and brought into focus in his death. The human response of love which the divine love evokes is governed by the will rather than the emotions however, and the element of obedience is prominent here as in Judaism and Islam. The Christian, like his Jewish and Muslim

---

[28]*Supra,* p. 89.

brother, is a man under authority. The Christian disciple is one who accepts the discipline of obedience to Christ, but as Professor Chalmers reminds us, "obedience to Christ must be expressed in the service of love."[29] And the corollary of love of God is love of neighbour.

This love is given visibility in the fellowship of the Church.[30] The Church is the primary Christian community, but it has a responsibility for the world as a whole. Since "the judgments of God are upon the whole earth", it assumes the prophetic task of relating the moral will of God to community relationships at both national and international levels. The Church proclaims and seeks to show that the way of love is the Way for all men; it is called to be an agency of reconciliation between men. Christianity is often charged with being divisive because of its exclusive claims, but it seeks to offer mankind a basis on which genuine community can be established, namely, reconciling love.

The implications of love for community might be more fully elaborated than they are in Professor Chalmers' chapter. Love includes a profound concern for freedom, for example; love has no meaning apart from freedom. But Christian freedom is neither the lonely rebellion of an atheistic existentialist nor the self-will of the rugged individualist; it is freedom-in-community. It is based on a recognition of the importance of choice, but even more fundamentally it is based on an acceptance of God's having chosen man, reflected in Christ's words, "You did not choose me, but I chose you."[31]

Though this has been interpreted by some in terms of a doctrine of election that offered freedom only to the "in-group", an adequate interpretation of love includes a profound concern for justice, justice for all men. Love may be regarded as the fulfilment of justice, but it may never be offered as a substitute for justice. This is to lapse into sentimentality. Justice must

[29]*Supra*, p. 94.

[30]*Supra*, p. 96.

[31]St. John 16:16.

rather be seen as a necessary instrument of love, as love seeks the welfare of all persons in community, rather than the few who may become the objects of charity. But unless love remains the norm and determining principle of justice, the latter may degenerate into injustice which gives less than is due to others, when their due is determined by the conviction that they are persons made in the divine image and bear the claim for fulfilment and participation in the redeemed community symbolized by the Kingdom of God. Or as Tillich puts it, "Justice is just because of the love which is implicit in it."[32]

This concern that the neighbour receive justice through love and love beyond justice is to be extended without reserve to the neighbour as neighbour, regardless of his willingness to accept the claims of Christ for his allegiance. In practice Christians fail too often to show love even to each other; the Church often offers sentimental togetherness rather than a genuine *koinonia*. Yet if there is one Christian value which ought to have universal relevance it is that of *koinonia* or community. As Gerald Cooke says, "In a day when men clutch at every type of human association which holds some promise of answering their need for personal and superpersonal acceptance and relatedness, the worshipping Christian community must not withhold one of its greatest gifts. If it would be true to its discipleship and apostleship its treasures must be shared now more than ever."[33]

It will be questioned whether Christian *koinonia* can be shared, whether this open acceptance and loving concern for the neighbour can be extended to those who cannot make the Christian confession. Can the Christian *koinonia* become real in any sense to those who accept neither the judgment nor the promise of him who is Lord of this community? The answer to this question is not simple. Certainly a Christian *koinonia* that is in any way complete is centred in the living relationship

[32]*Love Power and Justice* (New York: Oxford University Press, 1954), p. 15.
[33]*Op. cit.*, p. 176.

of its members with their Lord accepted in trusting faith and loving obedience. Yet this can never be a closed community; open acceptance and loving concern must ever be extended as far as possible beyond the confessing Christian community, in fulfilment of the demands of self-giving love for the neighbour. The Christians' Lord insisted that not even the enemy should be excluded from the disciples' self-giving love. Such love ought to provide an incomparable bond, making possible community transcending national, racial, religious and any other barriers between men.

ISLAM

For the Muslim, the meaning of life is defined in terms of submission to the will of God and serving as his deputy on earth. To serve as a deputy is "so to order his acts and his life as to realize in his human community the ideals which God has made known in his revelation. It is the practice of the principles laid down in the Qur'an for the good government of the ideal Islamic society."[34] These principles are also held to be applicable to universal society and are identified as unity and equality. All men have a common Creator, and thus differences of race, colour, nationality and class are superficial. "Mankind constitutes a single *umma*, nation, people or community."[35] Mankind's original unity in relation to God will finally be restored, and this is declared to be the function of Islam. Islam is offered as the universal religion which will constitute the fundamental basis of community or the unity of mankind.

The ideal of unity based on a common faith is not in fact realized, but it is given further support by what is described as "the cardinal doctrine of Muslim practice, the brotherhood of all believers." All who enter the Islamic fellowship do so as equal, first-class citizens. This is given concrete expression in

[34]*Supra,* p. 122.
[35]*Loc. cit.*

154

terms of equality before the law, which the Qur'an directs must be extended to non-Muslims living in a Muslim country.

A further basis of unity is unity of language, which is identified as Arabic. This strikes the non-Muslim and non-Arab as less than realistic, even with the author's recognition that "the full acceptance of the language as an international tongue must await the coming of the time when all men are more concerned with a world-wide community than with their private and national pre-occupations."[36]

Thus Islam offers principles—unity and equality—which are to apply to all mankind as a basis for community. The unifying factor is to be the Muslim faith, however, and the principles are in fact applied only within the Islamic community in terms of the direction given in the Qur'an and the Traditions. Equality of man means equality of believers,[37] and since all authority belongs ultimately to God, authority in the state belongs to members of the religious community. "Church and state . . . are one and the same."[38] Again, "It is not really possible to separate the thought of society in Islam from the thought of the state or the faith. All are inter-related, all are based on the one source, the Qur'an."[39]

It is evident that the meaning of life as here interpreted embraces a real concern for community: this is no individualistic faith. But if, as seems likely, the pattern of human community is increasingly to be pluralistic, it is difficult to find specific guidance here. Community is only envisaged in terms of the unity of the Islamic faith, and if the children of God are equal, it seems that Muslims are more equal than others. Nevertheless, the principle of man's equality before God and the sovereignty of God alone may have a fruitful application to the wider problems of world community; for the latter requires such principles to limit the pretensions of individual men and nations to absolute sovereignty. The Muslim emphasis on almsgiving is

[36]*Supra*, p. 125.
[37]*Supra*, p. 130.
[38]*Loc. cit.*
[39]*Supra*, p. 132.

significant in this connection. While this interpretation of the responsibilities of stewardship of the world's resources would need radical reinterpretation before satisfying twentieth century requirements of community life, the Muslim concept of alms-giving is to be understood as not fundamentally an act of charity but as the fulfilment of a community responsibility which must not be left to the individual conscience.

We have now examined the bearing of these representative religious interpretations of the meaning of life on the issue of community with a view both to identifying common ground and exposing differences. What conclusions can be drawn?

It would appear that the meaning of life in what may be called the religions of the Biblical God—Judaism, Christianity and Islam—is more integrally related to the concept of community than is the case with Hinduism and Buddhism. In Judaism, the meaning of life is focussed on the community-creating event at Sinai; in Christianity it is focussed on the community-creating Christ-event. In Islam, the prophet's new revelation issues in the *umma,* the new sacred community. On the other hand, the concept of community in these three religions has a particularity that has proven to be an offence to men of other faiths, whereas the non-biblical religions of Hinduism and Buddhism seem to lend themselves more readily to universalism. The *Gita* rejects any such concept as that of a chosen people in stressing the diversity of pathways that lead to the unity of truth. Those of us whose faith presents to others the "scandal of particularity" have a particular obligation to examine that faith in relation to the problem of contributing to a sense of universal human solidarity. Is it possible so to understand our faith that we may retain our particular commitments and loyalties without compromise, and yet at the same time not only show a tolerant respect for the faith of other men but be impelled to seek a greater measure of community of interest with them?

156

Those whose faith is particularistic will generally agree in rejecting any form of syncretism as a theologically unacceptable price to pay for world community. Even such liberals as Radhakrishnan, Hocking and Toynbee make it clear that while a world faith may be a desirable goal, yet men find form and meaning in their lives through particular faiths, and that an artificially constructed superreligion is not likely to provide a satisfactory substitute for these. If a world faith emerges, it will combine particularity and universality, Hocking insists. It should be added that liberals such as these regard the particular forms which religions assume as of secondary and relative importance, and are opposed by more orthodox Christian theologians such as Hendrik Kraemer who insist upon a unique revelation, based on what may be called "biblical realism." Yet while Kraemer repects any attempt to discover a universal essence underlying all religions, even he makes no absolute claims for man's religions including the Christian religion: all are imperfect instruments of man's religious consciousness and are in many ways relative to their cultural context. For Kraemer, however, as for most Christian theologians there is no question of the uniqueness and finality of the Christian revelation, as distinguished from and transcending any human construct whether cultural or religious. On the other hand it may also be said that Hindu philosophers often make comparable claims for the uniqueness and finality of Hinduism by virtue of its capacity to comprehend all religions, all approaches to the divine. What must be rejected is not a claim to uniqueness that springs from the heart of a given faith, but spiritual imperialism which militates against world community. Such imperialism tends to prevent the very encounter between men of different faiths which might conceivably issue in a more general recognition of the superiority of the truth claims of one of the faiths. What is called for is freedom for all to make a personal religious confession with integrity and conviction, in combination with an attitude of tolerant respect for other faiths.

157

Both dogmatic exclusiveness and dogmatic tolerance are to be avoided.

Professor R. L. Slater in a careful study entitled *World Religions and World Community* has argued that in fact, "the most prevalent type of religious community in the world today is that which expresses and maintains an outlook which may be described as *tolerantly* confessional.[40] He concludes that the great majority of religious people are "neither quite so close-minded nor so open-minded as might be the case if choice lay between the dogmatism encouraged by the one extreme and the roam-where-you-will relativism encouraged by the other extreme."[41]

This conclusion has a bearing on expectations in regard to world religions and world community in a number of respects. One of these is the inter-faith aspect. Professor Slater has demonstrated that there is evidence of confessional allegiance in all five of the great religions, including Hinduism; and he argues convincingly that this fact may well facilitate rather than prevent mutual understanding. Men of pledged loyalty who are to be found in all the great religions may respect each other for their very loyalty, for they recognize its significance in their own lives.

Again, it is held that where an aversion to dogmatic exclusiveness is maintained together with a definite allegiance to particular confessional symbols, religious forces are more likely to cooperate effectively in the interests of world community. Religious toleration is not in itself a sufficient instrument of community; the motivation of commitment is also required, which religion can provide. Religious conviction may be an instrument of division and often has been, but Professor Slater argues that it need not be. In what he has called the "symbol-confessional form of community," tolerance and genuine confession are united. Here, ultimate loyalties are defined by reference to symbols which transcend mere ideas and the rigidly

---

[40] New York and London: Columbia University Press, 1963, p. 206.
[41] *Loc. cit.*

defined ideologies which lend themselves to presumptuous intolerance and prevent any real coming together.[42]

Furthermore, the fact that the most widespread form of religious community is a confessional one which evokes particular loyalties is said to have a definite bearing on the *kind* of coming together in the name of religion which may be expected in the cause of world community. Particular loyalties may not prevent religious cooperation but they may rule out the possibility of one all-inclusive world religion which some have regarded as a precondition of world community.

An alternate possibility which should be noted is Hocking's concept of "reconception" as developed in *The Coming World Civilization*.[43] This lies in between the belief that one of the present world religions will displace the others and the view that all religions will be displaced by a new synthetic or syncretistic religion. (A synthetic religion is one which would take the differences between religions more seriously than in syncretism, but both presuppose a high degree of relativism.) Hocking proposes neither the abandonment of traditional affirmations nor their perpetuation in their present form. Rather, each of the living religious traditions will be reconceived in the light of new challenges such as the impact of other faiths, and new occasions such as the emergence of world community which Hocking regards as already well under way. In responding to these new factors in the world situation, men of the great religious faiths must reconsider their own traditions, and this will issue not in their abandonment but their enlargement. This process, Hocking believes, will result in the kind of growing together on a wide scale which is already evident on a small scale insofar as mystics of all religious traditions recognize each other.

---

[42]Professor Slater is here following the approach of Peter Munz in his *Problems of Religious Knowledge* (SCM, London, 1959), whose "symbol-adhering communities" seem to correspond to Slater's broad-confessional type of community which he has observed to be so widely prevalent. *Ibid*, p. 197.

[43]New York: Harper, 1956.

At this point however one is disappointed to find that important distinctions between different kinds of mysticism are blurred if not ignored. The concept of reconception may yet prove valuable, but Hocking's version of it has too many of the limitations of syncretism or synthesis to prove acceptable. We may find ourselves in more agreement however with his judgment that "the immediate vista for the coming civilization is that of a continued co-existence of at least a few of the great faiths."[44]

This presupposes the continued existence of religious pluralism at least for the foreseeable future, and surely a realistic appraisal of the prospects for world community must be based on an acceptance of this. Dr. Slater goes further and asks, "Is anything more required in the interests of world community than such a continued coexistence of the great faiths?—coexistence on this pattern of reciprocal and welcomed challenge".[45]

It is noted that Father John Courtney Murray in a recent analysis of religious pluralism in North America has suggested that his findings may be validly applied on a world scale.[46] While as a Roman Catholic he would prefer that his fellow Americans shared his religious commitment, yet as a Christian citizen he must consider what is in the best interests of the American community, given a religiously pluralistic situation. This pattern of the co-existence of different religious communities is likely to prevail and must be accepted as the context in which life is to be lived as we strive to strengthen the bonds of community. But more positively, Father Murray recognizes that good has come out of this pattern. It has not only supplied religious motivation, which as Hocking has maintained the state needs but cannot provide, but it has shown that religious pluralism (embracing Protestant and Roman Catholic, Jewish and secular groups) is compatible with political unity and

[44]*Ibid*, p. 154; quoted in Slater, op. cit. p. 217.

[45]*Loc. cit.*

[46]In *We Hold These Truths; Catholic Reflections on the American Proposition,* Sheed and Ward, New York, 1960.

stability. The continued health of this community depends on two things, according to Father Murray: a continuing dialogue between the religious groups as to how best to promote a common society that is "civil, just, free, peaceful, one,"[47] and a return to a natural law doctrine to provide the moral consensus necessary for a unified society.

Father Murray then extends the application of these considerations from religious pluralism in the United States to religious pluralism in the world. The structure of war that underlies the pluralistic society should be replaced by the more civilized structure of dialogue between coexistent religions. Thus "amid the pluralism a unity would be discernible—the unity of an orderly conversation."[48] Professor Slater in commenting on this point has noted that this is not an underlying unity such as Hocking finds but a unity *amid* the pluralism, based on a general acceptance of a natural law doctrine.

Protestant Christians and others will be less optimistic than Father Murray about the possibility of an inter-religious acceptance of a natural law doctrine. But the suggestion that there may be a ground of unity alongside grounds of difference, rather than seeking unity within difference in terms of some common essence may be a fruitful one, and the American pattern may be instructive. One aspect of the latter form of religious pluralism that would seem to be of particular value in a wider application is its emphasis on freedom. An essential instrument of this in the American situation is the doctrine and practice of separation of church and state. This does not mean that those who govern the community are unaffected by religious motivation, but rather that there shall be no interference by the state with any man's religious beliefs, no state demand for uniformity in religious belief. So conceived, religious pluralism is not merely tolerated as a necessary evil but valued as a condition of establishing a community of convinced believers, men who are free to believe and free also to criticize and receive

[47]*Ibid.*, p. 22.
[48]*Ibid.*, p. 24.

criticism from those who differ, and are thus enabled to grow toward an enlarged faith. There is some justification therefore for regarding religious pluralism as an instrument of community rather than an instrument of division; for it helps to give substance to freedom without which no meaningful community can be achieved. Freedom that is genuine will provide opportunities for all men to affirm and develop their religious and cultural traditions. Let each community of faith be true to itself, and let each community of faith be dynamic as it relates itself to our common stake in the new world community toward which we hope mankind is moving.

We submit then that as we seek to discover a spiritual foundation for world-mindedness, the most fruitful approach to the world religions will be to look not for some common essence but for what Father Murray has called unity amid difference. It may well be that the most important thing that different religious communities have in common is a clear and mutually recognized awareness of their differences, if this can be combined with respect for diversity. The importance of this is being demonstrated in the current encounter between Protestant and Roman Catholic Christians, and between Christians and Jews,[49] in which some who read this are now participating. It is also happening increasingly in the encounter between more diverse religious communities throughout the world as they become more authentically aware of each other through increased understanding of their own and each other's history.

But in addition to this, the various religious traditions have in common the fact that each and all are confronted by a common problem and responsibility, that of participating in the building of world community. As Professor Wilfred Cantwell Smith has put it, "This must be not only the kind of world in which we can all live together, but the kind also of which we can jointly approve, and to the building and sustaining of

[49]Cf. Solomon S. Bernards, "Theological Education for a Pluralistic Society" in *Encounter,* 1964, "the moral and spiritual health of the pluralistic society of which all of us are a part will depend to a significant extent on what we tell ourselves of each other."

which the faith of each can effectively inspire."[50] We have tried to show that within the various views of the meaning of life there are resources to support this kind of common venture, without dissolving significant differences.

Whether or not this can be achieved will depend of course not only on a general recognition of the kind of world this will be, but also on a general willingness to work toward that kind of community. This in turn will call for not only loyal commitment to one's own tradition, but at the same time for a willingness to enlarge one's understanding of one's own faith, the faith of others and of our common problems. Men of each tradition must ask themselves how their tradition can be developed in such a way as to contribute more effectively to world-mindedness while at the same time preserving its own integrity. Wilfred C. Smith suggests that the question is not "what is the role of each community in establishing compatibility, collaboration and brotherhood" but rather "what, through penitence and faith, may it become?"[51]

Finally, we presume to offer this further word to Christians for whom mission to others is both an essential ingredient of our faith and a frequent cause of offence: an acceptance of the fact of religious pluralism for the foreseeable future should not be a source of discouragement. The dialogue with men of other faiths must be engaged in only in ways which will engender mutual trust if we are to contribute to the common need for world community; but there is no reason why that dialogue should not be as persuasive as we can make it so long as we in turn are open to the persuasiveness of others. If there is risk in this, it is the price that has always been demanded of those who are serious in the pursuit of truth. The attempt to persuade will engender tension, but if it is made against the background of a common concern for community it should be a creative tension which will issue in something finer, both in our understanding of our own faith, our church and its mission,

[50]*The Harvard Divinity School Bulletin,* Vol. 29, No. 1, p. 16.
[51]*Ibid.,* pp. 13-14.

and in the nature of the world community which should emerge. It may indeed contribute significantly to the Christian mission by compelling Christians to dissociate their presentation of Christ from Western cultural interpretations, and thus allow him to speak most meaningfully and unambiguously to men brought up on other ways.

NOTES ON CONTRIBUTORS

RANDOLPH C. CHALMERS, B.A., B.D., Th.D., D.D., Professor of Systematic Theology and Philosophy of Religion, Pine Hill Divinity Hall, Halifax, N.S.; author of six books; editor of, and contributor to, five other books; contributor to religious journals.

EMIL L. FACKENHEIM, Ph.D., Professor of Philosophy, University of Toronto; ordained as Rabbi in Berlin, 1939; author of two books and numerous articles and reviews in philosophy and theology for various periodicals.

SHOYU HANAYAMA, M.A., Ph.D., Minister of Seabrook Buddhist Church, Seabrook, N.J., U.S.A.; formerly postgraduate and research work, University of Tokyo and Union Seminary, N.Y.; Research Associate University of Wisconsin.

JOHN B. HARDIE, M.A., B.D., Ph.D., Professor of Hebrew and Old Testament Literature, Pine Hill Divinity Hall, Halifax, N.S.; author of *The Mighty Acts of God*; contributor to journals and periodicals.

JOHN A. IRVING, M.A., Ph.D., Professor of Ethics and Social Philosophy, Victoria College, University of Toronto; author of three books; co-author and editor of several other works; contributor to scientific, philosophical and psychological journals.

C. DOUGLAS JAY, M.A., B.D., Ph.D., Professor of Religion and Christian Ethics, Emmanuel College, Victoria University, Toronto; contributor to religious journals.

P. NAGARAJA RAO, M.A., D.Lit. (from Benares Hindu University), Professor and Head of the Philosophy Department, Sri Venkateswara University, Tirupati, (A.P.), India; worked under the guidance of S. Radhakrishnan; author of *Introduction to Vedanta*.

M. RASJIDI, Graduate of Egyptian University and Docteur de l'universite (Paris), Associate Professor, Institute of Islamic Studies, McGill University, 1958-1963; formerly Indonesian Minister of State, Ambassador to Egypt and Saudi Arabia, Ambassador to Pakistan.

W. S. TAYLOR, M.A., B.D., Ph.D., D.D., Principal and Professor of Systematic Theology and Philosophy of Religion, Union College of British Columbia, Vancouver, B.C.; contributor to psychological and religious books and periodicals.

genuine Jew, the true Hindu, the authentic Muslim and the real Buddhist." Far from being on the defensive, the editors and contributors expound their distinctive positions with honesty and openness. Each contributor is a member of the faith about which he writes. Their conversation leads readily from "Encounter" to "Community."

Today's Christians especially are in a "Crisis of Meaning." In their encounter with other world religions they are obliged to "speak the truth in love" and carry on the dialogue. To help them, here is freedom of religious speech—ecumenical, truth-bearing, and eminently readable by eye, mind, and heart.

THE MEANING OF LIFE IN FIVE GREAT RELIGIONS

Edited by R. C. Chalmers and John A. Irving

THE RELIGION	MEANING OF LIFE	MORAL TEACHING	"LIFE-GOAL"
HINDUISM dates from the last centuries before the Christian era	*Life is "for man . . . to realize his full . . . potentialities . . . in his moral and spiritual life"*	*Follow the "road of morality"*	*The comprehension, through moral living, of the unity of all things*
BUDDHISM dates from the 6th century B.C. Buddha: born 563?, died 483? B.C.	*Life is following "the Four Noble Truths" which deal with and eliminate suffering*	*Walk in the Eightfold Right Path (Buddha's perfect way)*	*Nirvana, a state of tranquility, devoid of all suffering*
JUDAISM is usually dated from Abraham (about 2000 B.C.), or Moses (14th century B.C.)	*Life is a God-initiated meeting of man and God Who is the God of history acting and revealing Himself in the world*	*Obey the Mosaic Law and the teaching of the prophets*	*Obedience to the Law and the Prophets while awaiting the Messiah who will lead chosen Israel to inherit the earth*
CHRISTIANITY dates from Christ's birth and the first-century (A.D.) church	*Life is attaining a personal relation with God through the grace and truth revealed in Jesus Christ*	*The new commandment: "Love one another as I [Jesus Christ] have loved you" (John 13:34)*	*God's Kingdom on earth, as in "Thy kingdom come, thy will be done, on earth as it is in heaven"*
ISLAM is usually dated by Muhammad's life span: born 570, died 630 A.D.	*Life is submission to the Divine Will of one God, Allah, here on earth and in the life after death*	*Obey Allah's will as Muhammad's ethics and the Qur'an reveal it.*	*To live life always to the fullest, with the humble acceptance of what merciful Allah decrees*

RELIGION

THE WESTMINSTER PRESS®